10

Geoff Andrew

 Publishing

First published in 2005 by the
British Film Institute
21 Stephen Street, London W1T 1LN

The British Film Institute's purpose is to
champion moving image culture in all its
richness and diversity across the UK, for the
benefit of as wide an audience as possible,
and to create and encourage debate.

Series design by Andrew Barron
& Collis Clements Associates

Typeset in Italian Garamond
and Swiss 721BT by
D R Bungay Associates,
Burghfield, Berks

Printed in Great Britain by Cromwell Press

British Library Cataloguing-in-Publication Data
A catalogue record for this book is available
from the British Library

ISBN 0–85170–069–X

Contents

Acknowledgments

While this book represents a distillation of my own thoughts and feelings about *10*, it is, as always, partly the product of much informal discussion over the years with friends, colleagues and other Kiarostami fans. For insights, encouragement or help, I'd like to thank Gilbert Adair, Nick Bradshaw, Tom Charity, Michel Demopoulos, Alberto Elena, Simon Field, Thierry Frémaux, Jane Giles, Rose Issa, Nick James, Tareque Masud, Laura Mulvey, James Quandt, Tony Rayns, Jonathan Romney, Jonathan Rosenbaum, Walter Salles, Peter Scarlet, David Sin, Leopoldo Soto, David Thompson, Sheila Whitaker and Deborah Young. I should also like, once again, to thank my mother Olive and my wife Ane for their patience in dealing with my sometimes reclusive and obsessively single-minded behaviour during the preparation and writing of this book.

Since its publication coincides with a major London retrospective of Kiarostami's work, I should also thank Jim Hamilton, Julie Pearce, Waltraud Loges and other colleagues at the National Film Theatre; Margaret Deriaz, Erich Sargeant, Heather Stewart, Anthony Minghella and others at the British Film Institute; and, of course, Rob White – who proved an extremely sympathetic and helpful editor – and others at BFI Publishing. Their work is greatly appreciated.

This book could not have been written without further help from other Kiarostami aficionados. I should particularly like to thank Farhad and Majaneh Hakimzadeh of the Iran Heritage Foundation in London; Monica Donati and Marin Karmitz at MK2 in Paris; Mohammad Attebai in Tehran; and Elisa Resegotti, Alberto Barbera and Maria Grazia Girotto for their help at the Sulle Strade di Kiarostami exhibition in Turin.

Finally, I should very much like to thank Mania Akbari and, most especially, Abbas Kiarostami for their generous help in various matters. The book is dedicated to my wife Ane – who has watched, talked, lived and breathed Kiarostami with me for some years now – and to Abbas, who has taught me to look at cinema and life anew.

Unless stated otherwise, all quotations derive from interviews conducted by myself. The one with Mania Akbari took place in London in September 2002; those with Abbas Kiarostami took place in June 1999 in London (on stage at the National Film Theatre); in May 2002 in Cannes; in September 2003 in Turin; in January 2004 in London (one of them on stage at the Victoria and Albert Museum); and in May 2004 in Cannes.

1 Introduction: Something Small …

The reason I like this film is that even I, the film-maker, get confused as to which parts were fiction and which documentary. It's as if the film doesn't belong to me, as if it had made itself; the main character was so strong, it was I who was being told what should be done. And when I saw the film, I realised it was not an artificial creation, but different; it increased my responsibility as a film-maker. Cinema is no longer the panoramic experience it once was, with big budgets; cinema is – or ought to be – about analysing individual human experience, and how you can find yourself within that subjectivity. After making this film, I realised how I could identify with each of the characters, and how much of myself was in them …

Abbas Kiarostami[1]

Admirers of Kiarostami's *10* might imagine that the above quotation refers to that film. Actually, although the words are certainly applicable to *10*, the Iranian film-maker spoke them some years before he made it; that he was discussing *Close-Up* (*Namay-e nazdik*, 1990) suggests there is a degree of consistency in his work. And as soon as one examines the progress of Kiarostami's career in any detail, one gets an unusually strong impression of organic growth; as he himself has said, 'Every one of my films gives birth to another.'[2]

And that's crucial to a proper understanding of Kiarostami's achievements as a film-maker and, indeed, as an artist. All his films are perfectly comprehensible on their own terms as individual artefacts, but each becomes not only more accessible but richer and more resonant if

Seriously playful: Abbas Kiarostami and Amin Maher

one has an idea of its place within the context of his overall career. That, obviously, may be said about the work of many film-makers, but in Kiarostami's case the level of intertextuality is both extreme and extremely rewarding. In his perceptive and useful essay 'How to Read Kiarostami', Godfrey Cheshire rightly advises: 'Realize that the order you approach the films is crucial to how you understand them.'[3] Of course, one doesn't have to have seen each and every film Kiarostami has made in order to enjoy or understand *10*, and one certainly doesn't need to have encountered them all in the right order; it's rewarding, as with any other director, to 'fill in the gaps' when opportunities arise to see his earlier works. But if one is to get the most out of a Kiarostami film, it's often best to have at least some knowledge of its immediate predecessor and of the overall thrust of his career as director, especially as the 'meaning' of Kiarostami's films is often inextricably bound up with the aims, methods and circumstances of their making. In short, the more time you spend with Kiarostami's films, the more likely you are to get a lot out of them.

If this sounds like too much hard work to put into watching a movie – especially a 'little' movie like *10* – it shouldn't. For one thing, Kiarostami's films are not 'difficult'. Admittedly, their pacing may seem a little slow and their tone too quiet to those whose experience of cinema is limited to the wham-bam cutting and showy spectacle favoured by the Hollywood mainstream and its imitators for the last few decades. But the films do focus on recognisably ordinary humans and (mostly) tell some kind of story: Kiarostami's cinematic language has little to do with the cerebral theorising of a Godard, the religiose allegorising of a Tarkovsky, the erudite eccentricity of a Ruiz or the arcane mythologising of a Paradjanov. Indeed, praise for his films often mentions their naturalism and simplicity (the latter tending, naturally, to be somewhat deceptive). Accordingly, those who proclaim themselves non-believers regarding Kiarostami's mastery of film don't complain that the films are hard to understand; more damningly, they argue that there's nothing of interest in them anyway that needs to be understood.

When, for example, Roger Ebert reviewed *10*,[4] he began with a disingenuous confession – 'I am unable to grasp the greatness of Abbas Kiarostami' – before going on to claim that anyone could make such a film: 'Two digital cameras, a car and your actors, and off you go.' He argued that had the film been made in Europe or America instead of Iran – 'a country whose films it is somewhat daring to praise' – it would never have been accepted by the Cannes Film Festival (where it received its premiere); that 'no ordinary moviegoer, whether Iranian or American, can be expected to relate to his films'; that the films exist primarily for

'Two digital cameras, a car and your actors, and off you go…' Kiarostami and Mania Akbari 'on set'

festivals, critics and film students; and implied that Kiarostami's reputation depended on 'a cabal of dilettantes' (which, presumably, includes myself, since the review took me repeatedly to task for having praised *10* in *Sight and Sound*).[5]

Naturally, Ebert is not alone in his opinion, nor is distrust of the international acclaim won by Kiarostami's work to be found only among members of the popular press. In the fourth edition of his *Biographical Dictionary of Film*,[6] for example, David Thomson – coming (like many of us) a little late to Kiarostami, but with a more measured assessment than Ebert's – gently praises *The Taste of Cherry* (*Tam-e ghilass*, 1997) while venturing that he has seen the same kind of modernist take on neo-realism done before – and rather better – by Godard and many others. Furthermore, it's well known that in Iran many consider Kiarostami a relatively minor film-maker, inferior to Bahram Beyzai, Dariush Mehrjui and others, and reckon him probably guilty of making films designed to appeal primarily to Western viewers. This last charge was forcefully expressed by Azadeh Farahmand in an essay arguing, among other things, that a certain kind of Iranian cinema had found popularity among Western cinemagoers because its romantic depiction of an impoverished, rural country populated largely by children appealed to audiences anxious about the political instability between Iran and the Western powers.[7] Whatever the truth of this assertion (and leaving aside its questionable relevance to Kiarostami's oeuvre as a whole), Farahmand singles him out as someone whose elevated reputation in the West is a consequence of his sticking to 'safe' genres, by-passing censorable political issues and collaborating with foreign producers on films made for foreigners and festival directors rather than for his own people.

Certainly, one gets the impression that Thomson had perhaps not seen much of Kiarostami's work when he damned *The Taste of Cherry* with faint praise (conspicuously it's the only title he even mentions in his book's entry on the director); because the films build on and refine the achievements of their predecessors, Thomson may therefore have been writing – like anyone encountering the director's work for the first time – from a position of relative naiveté. Certainly, too, Farahmand's premise (admittedly, in a piece written before *10* was made) – that any film which doesn't explicitly criticise the socio-political situation in Iran is somehow 'safe' and automatically attractive to non-Iranian audiences – is nonsense, especially when applied to someone as unconventional and restlessly experimental as Kiarostami. Still, doubts about the purpose, significance and worth of his work do exist, and should be addressed. Hence this book.

It is, then, quite simply my contention that Abbas Kiarostami is one of the most important, audacious and rewarding film-makers currently at work, and that *10* – a defiantly 'small', ultra-low-budget film set entirely within the confines of one car, and made with two digital cameras, a tiny crew and a handful of non-professional actors – represents not only a landmark in his own career, but a lesson, offered by a master of cinema, which aims to demonstrate by way of example that there exists a fruitful way forward for a medium all too often characterised in recent years as moribund. Kiarostami has made numerous extremely fine films that would qualify as 'modern classics' worthy of inclusion in this series of books, and I am not sure that *10* represents his very greatest achievement;[8] nevertheless, it does occupy an intriguing and potentially very instructive position in its relationship to the mainstream cinema. As (or if) Kiarostami moves further from that mainstream in his continuing exploration of different modes of film-making (and film-watching), there will undoubtedly be others who adopt Ebert's argument that there is no real artistry to be found in his work. But, as I hope to demonstrate in the following pages, it is blinkered folly to dismiss *10* so easily: Kiarostami is seeking new ways to make us see and hear, feel and think. All we need do is open our eyes and ears, hearts and minds.

2 World Cinema at the Turn of the Millennium

In 1999, just two years after *The Taste of Cherry* had won the coveted Palme d'or at the celebrity-packed fiftieth edition of the Cannes Film Festival (it also went on to be selected as Best Foreign Film of the Year by the USA's National Society of Film Critics and Best Film of the Year by *Time* magazine), Kiarostami's next feature, *The Wind Will Carry Us* (*Bad mar-a khadad bord*, 1999) went on to win the Special Jury Prize and the FIPRESCI Award in Venice. The director had been collecting laurels for nearly three decades (his first short was fêted in Tehran in 1970, since when he'd notched up over fifty awards), but 1999 was a bumper year, with Turkey, Greece and France all honouring him with career-achievement gongs. At the turn of the decade he was voted best film-maker of the 90s in prestigious polls organised by the Cinemathèque Ontario and the American magazine *Film Comment*. Though he was unlikely ever to be given the thumbs-up by one of America's most famous and influential critics, Kiarostami was doing pretty well for himself.[9]

And even if, as Ebert and others have suggested, his films were appreciated only by Western festival directors and critics – a charge refutable partly by the good box-office performance of some of his films in certain territories, partly by the fact that he's also won prizes in cities as far apart as Singapore, São Paulo, Melbourne, Moscow and (very often) Tehran – would that make them less interesting or valuable? Not every film needs to be mainstream or populist; there's nothing inherently wrong in treating cinema as an art form in which one might experiment. (No one would suggest W. G. Sebald would have spent his time more wisely writing in the style of Jackie Collins, or that Miró should have turned to painting pretty landscapes or the illustration of comic books.) Why do some reviewers measure a film's worth partly according to its (prejudged) ability to please large numbers of people? That's surely not a matter of artistic value but commercial clairvoyance, yet it's now common practice – and it's deemed legitimate because the Hollywood dream factory has dominated the production, promotion and exhibition of films for three-quarters of a century. That's why, even today, many cinemagoers never consider cinema's potential as an art form – we're conditioned to think of it exclusively (if we're consumers) as entertainment or (if we're practitioners) as business. And too often art and entertainment are somewhat illogically deemed mutually exclusive.

By the 1990s, in fact, Hollywood seemed almost to have given up altogether on the idea of producing art. Industrial imperatives were obeyed virtually without question, so that, far more than before, the American mainstream devoted itself primarily to providing formulaic genre fare aimed at the young, complete with carefully moulded young stars as identification figures and dazzling special effects designed to accentuate the new, fantastic and spectacular. The characters and stories in these movies retreated ever further from life as any of us know it, yet the films, backed by the economic force of the conglomerates' marketing machines, exerted a stranglehold on the world's screens. Many welcomed the escapism, but others, frustrated by it, either stopped watching new films or began to look elsewhere for more authentic accounts of the world.

There'd always been alternatives. Over the decades, a number of national cinemas – Swedish, German, Russian, French, Italian and British included – had fought America's hegemony; some industries (notably in India, Egypt and Hong Kong) had even managed to lure locals away from Hollywood imports by producing spectacular home-grown genre fare themselves. But the difference, in the last decade or so of the 20th century, was that film fans prepared to venture beyond Hollywood and its mimics began to be offered – and to accept and enjoy – films from a far wider range of nations than those traditionally represented in art-houses and festivals. Once, Japan and India had been deemed the only Asian industries worth investigating, but by the turn of the millennium many found themselves watching films from China, Taiwan, Hong Kong, Thailand, South Korea, Iran, Turkey, Lebanon, Palestine and Israel; occasionally, even African movies made it on to European or American screens. Meanwhile, three decades after *cinema novo*'s heyday, people were enjoying crossover hits not only from Brazil but from Mexico and Argentina. Work by film-makers from Denmark, Austria, Greece, Belgium and Finland was reaching unexpectedly large audiences; and the first ever Inuit feature – the almost three-hour-long *Atarnajuat: The Fast Runner* (Zacharias Kunuk, 2000) – premiered to acclaim in Cannes before going on to enthral audiences wherever it played.

The climate had changed. Film-makers like Takeshi Kitano, Hou Hsiao-Hsien, Edward Yang, Wong Kar-Wai, Nuri Bilge Ceylan, Walter Salles, Alejandro González Iñárritu, Lars Von Trier, Michael Haneke, the Dardenne brothers, Aki Kaurismäki and others found themselves winning major prizes, reaching fair-sized audiences and being described in the same respectful terms as the established older auteurs. Thanks in part to protectionist policies of the kind castigated by Jonathan Rosenbaum in his book *Movie Wars*,[10] their work wasn't always distributed, exhibited or reviewed as it deserved but, to some at least, they proved that talk of the death of cinema was premature; that something interesting and exciting was definitely happening. Precisely *what* was happening and why were matters of debate; but there does seem to have arisen, in this age of mass migration, globalisation and new technologies, a curiosity about other societies. (Apart from anything else, since 11 September 2001, there also seems to have been an increased desire in many people to find out a little more about life in the Islamic world – presumably some want to gauge the accuracy of George W. Bush's 'Axis of Evil' rhetoric.) I'd also venture that some are tired of the limitations and evasions of so much Hollywood storytelling. The size-matters ethos promulgated by the dramatically infantile *Titanic* (James Cameron, 1997) and many other blockbusters, the cosy homilies proffered by the mainstream, and the apparently unshakeable belief held by some Hollywood film-makers that the capitalistic materialism of the American Dream is the be-all-and-end-all of modern life: all this has become rather wearisome. That's why the work of most of the directors listed above is attractive; they operate on a recognisably human scale, dealing not with fantastically heroic or romantic exploits but with something resembling everyday life, in all its messy complexity.

One more thing is worth mentioning. Shot in the Arctic wastes, *Atarnajuat*, like *10*, could not have been made without digital technology. To some extent, the very notion of world cinema is about empowerment: about people telling their own stories rather than simply accepting what Hollywood and its clones offer. Digital cameras, because they're comparatively small, inexpensive, portable, versatile, and able to record and store images in far greater quantities and in a far wider range of conditions than other cameras, play a crucial role in that empowerment. They aren't necessary or suitable for all kinds of film-making, but the technology is developing apace, and they'll be instrumental in shaping the future of cinema. In January 2004, Abbas Kiarostami told Londoners, 'There are about 6,000 people using digital cameras now in Iran. What's great is that they don't need to find a producer or money to make films. So I hope there'll be many interesting Iranian film-makers in the future.'[11]

3 Iranian Cinema: A Special Case

Of the national cinemas to have caught the attention of festival and art-house regulars over the last two decades, Iran has generated more excitement than most. In 1986, Amir Naderi's *The Runner* (*Dawandeh*) was released, winning international acclaim. Around the same time, Mohsen Makhmalbaf's *The Peddler* (*Dastforoush*) appeared, followed by *The Cyclist* (*Bicycle-ran*, 1987) and *The Marriage of the Blessed* (*Arusi-ye khuban*, 1988). And in 1989 Kiarostami's *Where Is the Friend's House?* (*Khaneh-ye dust kojast?*, 1987) carried off five prizes at the Locarno Film Festival; three years later, after *Close-Up* had won a clutch of awards around the world, he had a film for the first time at Cannes. Not only was *And Life Goes On…* (*Va zendegi edameh darad*, 1992) judged Best Film in the Un Certain Regard strand, but Kiarostami was honoured with the Roberto Rossellini Award for his career overall. Some of the world's cinemagoers, it seemed, were ready to take an interest in Iranian cinema, and over the next decade or so the number of Iranian films playing abroad grew from a slow trickle to a very steady stream.

There are a few theories as to why Iranian films caught the imagination of foreign audiences at this time. Jonathan Rosenbaum has argued that Iran was so demonised in the West as a dangerous fundamentalist state after the Islamic Revolution of 1978–9 – and especially after the American Embassy hostage crisis of 1979–81 – that people wanted to look beyond the stereotypes of fanaticism proffered by the news media.[12] Others take this idea further, arguing to the effect that there is a patronising, exoticist or sadistic element to the interest some Westerners take in seeing images – also stereotypical – of impoverished rural communities and suffering women.[13] But while there may be some truth in both of these explanations, neither, surely, is sufficient in itself, since each fails to take into account the quality of the films themselves.

Many of the Iranian films released abroad have boasted an approach to cinematic storytelling that is dazzlingly visual and sometimes daringly eloquent in its use of certain formal tropes; at the same time they often display a heart-felt humanism seldom found in Western films. Indeed, one of the appealing aspects of Iranian cinema may have been its intriguing blend of traditional and modern elements. Godfrey Cheshire has argued that the relative isolation of Iran since the Revolution may have had unexpected but rewarding consequences. Pointing out that Iranian film-making in the 70s was marked by a cinematic modernism that had come to the fore in Europe in the 50s and 60s, he continues:

What is uncommon, and peculiar to Iran, is how that aesthetic was preserved virtually intact for future decades … While the rest of the world was swept up in an increasingly globalized and video-dominated media climate, Iran shut off almost everything coming from the outside, and then, circa 1983, encouraged its film-makers to resume their former preoccupations (albeit with new restrictions on content). Thus did the modernist-cinematic 60s/70s survive to enjoy a vital afterlife …[14]

(This argument applies only to post-Revolutionary art cinema; as Hamid Naficy explains,

… two cinemas have developed side by side. The 'populist cinema' affirms post-revolutionary Islamic values more fully at the level of plot, theme, characterization, portrayal of women and mise-en-scène. The 'art cinema', on the other hand, engages with those values and tends to critique social conditions under the Islamic government.[15]

As *10* belongs to the second group, it's the development of that strain we shall examine briefly here.)

The modern Iranian art cinema began, tentatively, in the late 50s and early 60s when, as an alternative to the popular melodramas and musicals, a number of films were made depicting Iranian life in more realistic terms, among them *The House Is Black* (*Khaneh siyah ast*, 1962), a short documentary about a leper colony by the acclaimed poet Forough Farrokhzad, which Kiarostami has cited as an influence on his work. (He also used a line from one of her poems for the title of *The Wind Will Carry Us*, and has a character recite the entire poem in the film.) Nevertheless, the regime of Shah Mohammad Reza Pahlavi greeted any films it deemed critical of contemporary Iran with disapproval or censorship, and not until 1969, when Dariush Mehrjui had an unexpected hit with *The Cow* (*Gav*) – a stark, sardonic account of village life – did any momentum build up. Around this time, numerous important directors began making films, including Ebrahim Golestan, Bahram Beyzai, Amir Naderi, Parviz Khimiavi and Sohrab Shahid Saless, whose *A Simple Event* (*Yek Ettefaq-e sadek*, 1973) has also been acknowledged as an influence by Kiarostami; he himself, as we shall see later, also embarked on his film career at this time, for the Institute for the Intellectual Development of Children and

"My night so brief is filled
with devastating anguish.

Young Adults (Kanun). The pro-Western Shah, meanwhile, was
encouraging a more international appreciation of cinema, both through
the Shiraz Art Festival (a determinedly modern event established in 1968,
which brought to Iran figures like Peter Brook, Shuji Terayama and
Karlheinz Stockhausen) and through the Tehran International Film
Festival, which was established in the early 70s and introduced subtitled
versions of foreign-language films to the capital.[16]

But cinema has been viewed ambivalently in Iran ever since the early
1900s when Muslim clerics declared themselves opposed to the
representation of the human face and body on screen.[17] By 1978, with
anti-Pahlavi demonstrations becoming more frequent and more heated,
cinemas were seen by many of the exiled Ayatollah Khomeini's supporters
as examples of Iran's cultural colonisation and corruption by the West. In
August of that year, more than 300 people were burnt to death when the
Rex cinema in Abadan was set alight by anti-Shah militants; by the time
Khomeini and the government of the Islamic Republic were in place the
next year, some 180 cinemas had been destroyed or closed down.[18] No
wonder Kiarostami and his film-making compatriots take the ethical
responsibilities of their chosen profession more seriously than many of
their Western counterparts.

Not that there was much opportunity to work in the years immediately
following the Revolution. With the outbreak of the Iran-Iraq War in 1980
following hard upon the severance of diplomatic ties with the USA, the
Islamic government introduced repressive measures to reduce opposition
to the theocracy. Intellectuals and dissidents were jailed or executed,
universities closed, newspapers shut down, and women subjected to
severe regulations of dress and behaviour. Many Iranians went into exile,

Shadows in paradise: *The Wind Will Carry Us* (MK2 Productions, 1999) and what film-making was allowed was seen by the authorities – if not by the film-makers – as an opportunity for propaganda. As Naficy points out, 'The clerical leaders were not opposed to cinema per se; they were against what Ayatollah Khomeini called its "misuse" by the Pahlavi regime to corrupt and subjugate Iranians.' [19]

Accordingly, in 1982 the Ministry of Culture and Islamic Guidance was charged with the enforcement of a code of regulations governing exhibition (Mohammad Khatami, later President, first made his mark in the ministry). A set of regulations was drawn up,[20] and the following year the ministry established the Farabi Cinema Foundation to control the import and export of films, and encourage and oversee production; cinema had been Islamicised, in theory if not in practice. The number of films being made rapidly increased, with the result that Beyzai found success again with *Bashu, the Little Stranger* (*Bashu, Gharibeh-ye kuchak*, 1985), Naderi with *The Runner* and Mehrjui with *The Tenants* (*Ejareh-neshin-ha*, 1986). Around the same time, Mohsen Makhmalbaf was establishing himself as the most notable of the directors who made their first films after the Revolution, while Kiarostami was preparing to make his third feature. (*The Traveller* [*Mosafer*, 1974] and *The Report* [*Gozaresh*, 1977] had been made while the Shah was in power.) There was an opportunity for some kind of renaissance, and Iran's film-makers made the most of it.

They did, however, have to work under severe constraints. In terms of exhibition there were far too few cinemas left to cater for a rapidly growing urban population, and many were in decrepit condition and relied on poor equipment. The availability of cheap satellite dishes had also taken its toll on exhibition. But the major problem facing film-makers

Spite marriage: *The Report*

remained censorship. More limiting, in the long term, than the guidelines dealing with the treatment of Islam, the Republic and Iranian history were the strict regulations concerned with the depiction of women. It was not merely a matter of showing Muslim women as chaste, God-fearing wives and mothers; as Naficy says, a new visual grammar of film evolved regarding *hejab* (modesty). It was applied to women's physique and positioning (no attention should be drawn to their 'provocative walk'), their gaze (eye contact with men was discouraged, and as men were also in the audience, close-ups to be avoided) and their dress, particularly the *chador* (the veil or scarf worn by Muslim women to conceal their hair).[21]

At first women were merely background presences, barely functional in any story, but by the late 80s film-makers (including a few women like Rakhshan Bani-Etemad and Tahmineh Milani) were giving female characters more prominence. Even so, because the regulations essentially treated not only the male actors but also the audience as if they were actually in the film or on set, female characters had to dress and behave throughout as if they were in the presence of non-related men. This resulted in on-screen behaviour that was transparently a distortion of its real-life equivalent: an on-screen husband and wife, for example, would avoid physical and eye contact, and wives and mothers would wear a *chador* even in the privacy of their on-screen home. And because women were never to be seen as sexual beings, stories and situations involving desire and love were avoided. As Mohsen Makhmalbaf explained, these rules created real problems for film-makers:

Suppose in your screenplay you are showing the private life of a husband and wife. If the woman covers her face really well because of the presence of spectators, this action would indicate either a lack of intimacy or the existence of a dispute, and naturally in real life something like this would not occur. If we want to show them walking around ... as though they are husband and wife, then it becomes un-Islamic because spectators are unrelated to that woman.[22]

Notwithstanding these and other restrictions, Iranian film-makers found ways of telling stories that somehow made sense, and during the 90s, their films began to appear in ever greater numbers at international festivals. In Iran itself, censorship and the struggle between liberals and conservatives continued: in 1992, a year after a debate over what rightists called a 'cultural invasion' by Western imperialism, Khatami resigned from his post as Minister of Culture and Islamic Guidance; in 1997, in a landslide victory in which his reformist manifesto received massive support from Iran's swelling young population, he was elected President of the Islamic Republic.[23] Any hopes that he would rid Iran of its strict laws, however, have proved largely groundless, and many complain that the reform movement has lost its momentum. But at least Iranian cinema has gone from strength to strength on the international front, with several directors now established as major talents.

Apart from Kiarostami himself, Mohsen Makhmalbaf has probably proved most influential, partly through his own films – which include *Salaam Cinema* (1994), *Moment of Innocence* (*Nun va goldun*, 1995), *Gabbeh* (1996) and *Kandahar* (*Safar-e Qandehar*, 2001) – and partly through the Makhmalbaf Film House, a kind of film school from which various members of his family have graduated, most notably daughter Samira who, after precociously making a splash with *The Apple* (*Sib*, 1998), *Blackboards* (*Takhteh-siah*, 2000) and *At Five in the Afternoon* (*Panj-e asar*, 2003), may see her fame eclipse that of her father. Majid Majidi looked set for a while, with *Children of Heaven* (*Bachecha-ye aseman*, 1997) and *The Colour of Paradise* (*Ranghe-khoda*, 1999) to find commercial success, though both these films, with their sweet, sentimentally uplifting tales of children overcoming obstacles, seem carefully calculated Kiarostami-lite mediocrities compared to most recent Iranian fare. A far more rewarding director, for instance, who also happens to make films about children is Abolfazl Jalili; to films like *Don* (*Daan*, 1997), *Dance of Dust* (*Raghs-e-khak*, 1998), *Delbaran* (2001) and *Abjad* (2003), Jalili has brought compassion, a tough sense of injustice, and a near-abstract sense of visual poetry. Then there is Jafar Panahi, a former assistant to Kiarostami, who first came to the world's notice with *The White Balloon*

High and low:
Crimson Gold

Camera buff: *The Day of the Premiere of 'Close-Up'* (Nanni Moretti, 1996)

(*Badkonak-e sefid*, 1995). Based on a script by his mentor, this charming film suggested Panahi might be a reliable *metteur en scène* with little to say for himself – an erroneous impression corrected when both *The Circle* (*Dayereh*, 2000) and *Crimson Gold* (*Tala-ye sorgh*, 2003) – the latter again from a script by Kiarostami – showed he was expert at maintaining a tense, even nightmarish mood, and passionately concerned about social inequality.

There have of course been many other fine Iranian films in recent years, but the above are arguably the most important and interesting Iranian directors to have come to the fore in the last decade or so. None, however, has been showered with as much praise as Abbas Kiarostami – not only by critics, festival directors and (*pace* Ebert) 'ordinary' cinemagoers, but by an extraordinarily diverse range of film-makers, including Kurosawa, Godard, Scorsese, Chahine, de Oliveira, Angelopoulos, Bertolucci, Rosi, Erice, Moretti, Herzog, Breillat, Haneke, Kitano, Kaurismäki, Salles, Hodges, Philibert, Wenders, Egoyan, Kusturica, Ripstein, Schroeder, Tarantino … The list is seemingly endless.[24] And since, as was stated earlier, Kiarostami's films grow out of, build upon and reflect back on their predecessors, we should, before turning to *10*, take a brief look at his work prior to that film.

4 Abbas Kiarostami: A Very Special Case

Abbas Kiarostami was born in Tehran on 22 June 1940; his father was a decorator, and the family was large. By his own admission, he was shy and a poor student at school, where he developed an interest in painting; he has said it helped him cope with loneliness. Leaving home at eighteen, he found work as a traffic cop, and continued in that job (and then in a desk job in the city's traffic offices) after gaining a place in the Faculty of Fine Arts at the University of Tehran. By the time he graduated, he had decided he'd never make a good painter; he'd developed an interest in graphic design, however, and began work as a commercial artist, designing book covers, posters and, eventually, film credits sequences and advertisements. He seems to have enjoyed his work; he made over 150 commercials between 1960 and 1969, and has spoken of the pleasure he took from

the minimalist aspect of graphic design ... It is an art that communicates to the general public with the minimum of means and the maximum of constraints ... Working in this domain is a good exercise for creating methods of communication without using the habitual tools.[25]

He did, however, feel frustrated by commercial considerations taking precedence over creative ones, and in 1969 accepted an invitation from his friend Firuz Shirvanlu to work at Kanun. Initially, he was to illustrate a children's book by the poet Ahmad Reza Ahmadi,[26] but thanks to his experiences in advertising and the film world, he was asked to help set up Kanun's film department. He ran the unit for five years; more relevant to our purposes, however, is that after about a year Kiarostami made his own first film for Kanun. In *Bread and Alley* (*Nan va koucheh*, 1970), a twelve-minute black-and-white short of great imaginative concision, a small boy making his way home from the bakery is too afraid to walk past a barking dog – until he tries giving it bread, at which point the dog, tail wagging, follows him home and sits waiting outside. Then the next nervous infant appears ...

This modest little gem anticipates much of Kiarostami's work in various respects. Obviously, like most of his films up to and including *Where Is the Friend's House?* and the documentary *Homework* (*Mashq-e shab*, 1989), it features children (he was working for Kanun, after all) and is faintly didactic. (That said, as with most of its successors, it is never remotely 'preachy', and it's difficult to say with any certainty just what

The journey begins: *Bread and Alley*

lesson we are supposed to take away from it, other than that it's best when facing a problem to use one's brain rather than panic or give up.)[27] Moreover, it takes a journey as its structural basis; it leavens its (modicum of) drama with humour as it charts the protagonist's efforts to overcome a challenge; it makes inventive, expressive use of sound (the jolly jazz cover of The Beatles' 'Ob-La-Di, Ob-La-Da' playing over the credits as the boy walks happily home comes dissonantly to a close – as if a record player had been suddenly unplugged – when he encounters the barking dog); it makes likewise effective use of some unusually long takes; and it includes several moments which most other directors would probably dismiss as 'dead time', as when the boy just waits, wonders what to do, wipes his nose, listens a while, and waits some more.

Perhaps most surprising, however, is the way the film plays with point of view, especially in the final moments. Despite some lovely digressions involving passers-by, we assume from the start that the film's about the child; the dog's bad (and not human) so we identify with the boy. But when we see the dog follow the boy home, we realise it's a stray and probably hungry, poor thing. So as the boy goes inside, leaving the now nice-looking mutt on the step, our allegiances shift … till a still younger lad enters the street and the dog sits up and barks. At this point, are we to feel relieved for the first boy, sorry for the stray, be impressed by its strategic cunning, or worry about the new kid on the block? He has no bread, after all … Kiarostami's freeze-frame of a frightened face is an unusually open ending, leaving us no room for complacency, but plenty for confusion, concern and contemplation.

All this is unusually rich pickings for a first short, yet the abiding impression left by the film is of simplicity. Kiarostami often jokes that the boys, the old man, the dog and the director were all non-professionals, and this, combined with the linear purity of what's no more than a narrative vignette (or a philosophical problem in need of a practical solution), gives the film an aura of spontaneity and freshness. It is also, given many potential pitfalls, remarkably free of cuteness and sentimentality. In all these respects it anticipates not only Kiarostami's subsequent shorts for Kanun but his first feature, made three years later, again in black and white. (Since then he has worked almost exclusively in colour.)

The Traveller is typical of much of his work in that it turns a simple journey into a full-blown if rather meandering quest. (Even in *Bread and Alley* the journey was physical *and* metaphorical, in terms of the boy's character and consciousness.) Again the 'hero' is a boy, a football fanatic in his early teens who determines, against all the odds, to travel to Tehran to see an international match; again, too, mawkishness is rigorously avoided. The boy, apart from being a no-hoper at school, is quite happy to get his bus fare by stealing from his parents and conning his classmates with a scam in which they pay him to take photographic portraits with a camera he knows is defunct; moreover, when he eventually makes it to the stadium, he's so exhausted that he falls asleep, has a nightmare in which he's beaten up,[28] and wakes to find he's missed the entire match. To Kiarostami, it barely matters that neither the object nor the methods of the boy's obsessive quest are worthy; what counts is his spirit, determination and a cunning, almost entrepreneurial intelligence of which his teachers and parents seem entirely unaware. Not that these enable him to see the game. But while he experiences a sense of failure that's vivid enough in the last, bleak shots of the now empty, litter-strewn stadium for the viewer also to feel cheated (and chastened – why did we root for this boy?), the film is structured in such a way that we remain aware that what counts is not the end but the means: the whole journey we've just witnessed, even if it led 'nowhere'.

As Jonathan Rosenbaum has pointed out, *The Traveller* relies more heavily on narrative and is closer to traditional neo-realism than most of Kiarostami's films.[29] Still, anyone new to his work might be surprised not only by the downbeat ending but by a delicious disruption that occurs when the story suddenly just stops for a minute or two so that we can sit back and enjoy a beautiful (but not 'cute') montage of boys posing for a stills camera which, in terms of the narrative 'reality', will never record their expressions. But Kiarostami's camera could record them, of course, and he generously shares what he captured, allowing us time, encouraging

Working towards a goal: *The Traveller*

us to look, and *see*. Even more surprising to the newcomer, however, might be Kiarostami's use of repetition in the narrative: a device he would thereafter develop – for humour or dramatic emphasis, for comparison or contrast, or whatever – in such a way that it became one of the hallmarks of his style.

He used it in his next short, *Two Solutions for One Problem* (*Do rah-e hal baray-e yek masaleh*, 1975), to illustrate, with an almost surreal slapstick humour, the benefits of rational co-operation over irrational conflict. After a boy borrows and accidentally tears a friend's notebook, a mildly retaliatory response sets off an escalating storm of violence in which the boys' possessions and clothes are laid waste; an animated blackboard then tots up the scores – a futile draw – in their grudge match, before we see a replay in which the book is repaired and forgiveness and friendship prevail. A similar structure was used to reflect on issues of loyalty, betrayal and responsibility in a rarely seen documentary made at the time of the Revolution, *Case No. 1, Case No. 2* (*Ghazieh shekel avval, ghazieh shekel dovvom*, 1979), and again in the extraordinary short *Orderly or Disorderly* (*Be tartib ya bedun-e tartib*, 1980). Here, Kiarostami is apparently offering a didactic study of how disciplined behaviour is more efficient than undisciplined activity; he shows children, for example, getting on a bus in random fashion and then doing the same thing in file and slightly more quickly, at which point he concludes (in off-screen voiceover) that order is better. But by the time he's applied this parallel narrative structure to a few more case studies – such as cars at a busy intersection in Tehran – the message is murkier: it's not only harder to prove order's more efficient, but there's also a suggestion that the film-makers are actively influencing the 'objective' reality they first seemed simply to be documenting. This brief masterpiece – which, like Kiarostami's next short

The Chorus (*Hamsorayan*, 1982), shows his enduring interest in experimenting with the relationship of image to sound – is at once delightfully anarchic fun and a brilliant exploration of the way film-making and 'reality' affect one another.

Perhaps the most extreme use of repetition occurs in *Fellow Citizen* (*Hamshahri*, 1983), a documentary about a traffic cop trying to stop drivers from going down a street in the centre of Tehran. For almost an hour all we see and hear are his conversations with countless drivers explaining why they should be treated differently from everyone else; the repetition is made still more apparent by the fact that most of the film is shot, with a telephoto lens of which the drivers are unaware, from a single angle. The effect of this in many ways minimalist strategy is both emphatic and amusing; the film not only evokes a society on the brink of chaos (almost everyone appears ready to put him or herself above the public good), but shows and celebrates, often very funnily, man's astonishing capacity for narrative invention – or, to put it bluntly, for lying.

A more honourable aspect of human endeavour was the subject of *Where Is the Friend's House?* This was Kiarostami's first international success, and while it's a very beautiful film, full of subtle nuance, its 'uplifting' tale – of a boy's sterling efforts to return a homework notebook to a fellow pupil who's been threatened with expulsion and who lives somewhere on the other side of a mountain from the hero's home – has done more, perhaps, than any other film to foster the mistaken notion that Kiarostami is a sentimental humanist in the realist tradition, pure and simple. Not only is the film far darker than this synopsis suggests, particularly in its account of how adults exploit and ignore children, but it's by no means the straightforward neo-realist work it first seems. The rural 'reality' on view was substantially modified by Kiarostami (famously, he built the zigzagging hillside path shown repeatedly as the hero runs back and forth in search of his friend, while the after-dark scenes in the village are shot so as to create a partly magical, partly nightmarish mood); moreover, the repetitive, ritualistic aspects of the boy's odyssey emphasise its poetic and philosophical dimensions. Taking its title from a poem by Sohrab Sepehri, the film deploys traditional Persian symbols (the snaking path, a solitary tree on a hill, a flower, etc.)[30] to relate an ethical parable about the necessity and the difficulty of making the right choices and acting accordingly; in short, the journey gives the boy a lesson in life.

If anyone expected the film's success to result in more of the same, they were mistaken; while Kiarostami's films grow out of their predecessors, he seldom proceeds in linear fashion but tends to follow a

Life-lessons: *Where Is the
Friend's House?*

fittingly zigzag-like course. So while *Homework* again dealt with what
schoolkids did in the evenings, and whether their parents punished them,
it took a very different approach. A documentary consisting mainly of
repetitious face-on interviews with boys at a junior school, the film
(explained by an off-screen Kiarostami, in response to kids' queries, as a
research project prompted by problems his own son was having with
homework) offers a critique not only of an education system which makes
children learn by rote (rather than develop their curiosity, enthusiasm and
understanding), but of the intellectual neglect and physical punishment
many children suffer at home. But what's special about the film is how
Kiarostami makes his own role in it transparent: not only are the
interviews intercut with reverse-angle shots of himself and his cameraman
facing us/the camera (which, we should perhaps assume, is how the often
frightened or nervous interviewees saw them), but we get a sense of how
he's shaping the material, as when – purportedly out of respect for the
authorities because the pupils in the playground are not reciting anti-Iraqi
war-chants properly – he turns off the sound, and turns another example
of attempted mass indoctrination into comic spectacle. This, emphatically,
is not like the grandstanding practised by Nick Broomfield or Michael
Moore; far from playing the hero, Kiarostami is simply reminding us that
this is in no sense 'objective reality' but something shaped in subtle,
complex ways during and by the film-making process.

His next film, *Close-Up,* went about as far as it's intelligibly possible to
go in exploring the tangled relationship of a film, the film-maker, the
audience and 'reality'. Ostensibly making a documentary on the true story
of Hossein Sabzian – an impoverished film fanatic on trial for fraud after
he led a family to believe he was Mohsen Makhmalbaf and received

money from them on the understanding that they'd appear in his next film – Kiarostami fragments his narrative into so many diverse strands that we're made to question a range of assumptions about truth and falsehood, reality and representation. Hossein and the Ahankhah family 'play' themselves, as do Kiarostami, Makhmalbaf and the judge in whose courtroom some of the action takes place. But while it *looks* as if we're watching the trial, might not what we see be a dramatic reconstruction (especially given that the off-camera Kiarostami asks as many questions as the judge)? After all, other scenes recreate what (someone or another said) took place. But then why, when two policemen accompany a journalist to the Ahankhahs' to collect Sabzian, do we stay outside with the cab driver? Why, instead of a presumably dramatic arrest, are we left watching someone apparently irrelevant to the story in hand, who's simply at a loose end, walking around and distractedly kicking an old aerosol can so that it rolls zigzagging down the street?

The point, of course, is that it's impossible to know anything for certain; there are things we're not witness to, motives we cannot fathom, and lies that illuminate the truth. *Close-Up* is not only *about* lies; as a film attempting to do the impossible and reproduce reality, it tells plenty, too. But by acknowledging its own fallibility and falsehoods, it does in fact come a little closer to the truth – just as we, finally, are left sure of one thing alone: that Hossein Sabzian – who certainly misled the Ahankhahs by passing himself off as a famous film director, and who consequently got to be in a movie for real, playing himself playing Makhmalbaf for another famous film director, and who actually got his 'victims' into a film as well, as promised – is human, and therefore a complex, mysterious soul deserving of our respectful attention.

The real filmmaker and the fake filmmaker: Mohsen Makhmalbaf and Hossein Sabzian in *Close-Up*

Close-Up made it clearer than ever that Kiarostami's special area of interest was a fertile no-man's-land located somewhere between documentary and fiction; indeed, he has confessed he sees no real difference between them. For *And Life Goes On …*, shot a year after a massive earthquake had devastated the mountainous region that served as the setting for *Where Is the Friend's House?*, he recreated (though *not* as documentary) the journey he'd made immediately after the quake to see if the villagers cast in that film had survived. The movie, which has someone play the Kiarostami surrogate rather than have the director appear as himself, is a landmark in his oeuvre for several reasons. It's the first (if we except *Fellow Citizen*) to make extensive use of a car, and introduces what became a trademark shot: a vehicle observed in long shot crawling along serpentine mountain roads while we hear, as if off-screen, the conversation of the unseen people inside. It's the first to refer back *explicitly* to a predecessor. It's the first to end with a suspenseful shot which – due to its composition, duration or lighting – denies narrative information we expect to be provided and which most other film-makers would deem crucially important. (Here, we never get to see the two boys the director says he's most eager to see again.)[31] And finally, and most interestingly in terms of the film being something of a turning-point in his career, while the film again deals with the relationship of children and adults (the director is accompanied by his son), it's the first of Kiarostami's films about death being a constant, unavoidable presence in life.

Not that that theme was especially foregrounded in *Through the Olive Trees* (*Zir-e derakhtant-e zeytun*, 1992), his third film set in the Koker region, and therefore seen by many as the final instalment of an unplanned 'Koker Trilogy'.[32] It's notable mainly for taking the self-reflexive strategy of its predecessor a step further, in that we now have an actor (who opens the film by telling us he's an actor) playing the director of *And Life Goes On …* at the time of its making: among other things, this film recreates the shooting of a scene which featured a newly wed couple, the irony being that the actors involved are not married but the boy adores the girl, who refuses to indicate whether she's interested – which naturally makes filming troublesome, as 'reality' keeps intruding. It's all very witty, poignant and modernist – at one point the notably unobservant Kiarostami surrogate is seen talking to the Kiarostami surrogate from *And Life Goes On …*! – but what makes the film more than just a pleasingly playful in-joke and love story remains the earthquake, and how it has affected the people on view.

Really a fake: one of the two Kiarostami surrogates seen in *Through the Olive Trees* (who has also appeared, as a Kiarostami figure, in *And Life Goes On …*)

By now, Kiarostami was clearly a world-class film-maker to be reckoned with, and *The Taste of Cherry*, his first film in Cannes' main competition, shared the top prize.[33] Not that it could be considered a calculated attempt to make him a household name; it is one of his most austere, uncompromising works, set mostly inside a car. A middle-aged man drives around the dusty, sun-scorched hills on the edge of Tehran, first inspecting the men at the roadside and offering some of them a lift (it takes a while to find out why), and then trying to persuade three such passengers, in succession, to help him commit suicide by checking, the morning after he's taken some sleeping pills and settled down in a ditch, whether he's still alive; if not, he should be buried. A taxidermist reluctantly agrees, and that night the man, going alone to his resting place, lies down to look at the black sky …

A film of magnificent, sombre beauty, *The Taste of Cherry* made more audacious use of repetition and ellipsis than any Kiarostami film since *Close-Up*. Forcing viewers to fathom for themselves what his protagonist was doing and why, he denied them a proper identification figure, and even refused to satisfy any desire to know whether the suicide attempt is successful: the 'story' proper ends with a shot of the night sky and the sound of rain, before we see grainy video footage of the shoot, with Kiarostami, his lead actor and some soldiers seen earlier as extras relaxing on the hill; as Louis Armstrong's funereal 'St James Infirmary' plays on the soundtrack, we see the actor is alive but know nothing about his character's fate. But we do, surely, recall arguments used by his passengers in favour of life; the taxidermist's, especially, about the ephemeral pleasures of life – a taste of mulberries or cherries – linger in the memory, alongside the driver's anguished gaze.

Who served your father his tea?

That close, unsettling juxtaposition of life and death recurs in *The Wind Will Carry Us*, but is this time given considerably lighter, more comic expression. From the opening long shots of a car careering along country roads, with the invisible driver and passengers wondering which single tree on a hillside will direct them to the remote Kurdish village that is their destination, it's clear Kiarostami is in playfully enigmatic mood. The TV crew has come, secretly, to film a taboo and ancient ritual of the village's womenfolk, which they expect soon to occur when an ailing hundred-year-old dies. The trouble for them is, she just keeps on hanging on; the trouble for us is, we see only one of them (let's assume he's the director), we never see the old woman, and most of the other characters aren't shown either, even when they're heard – by the director alone on his mobile, or by us too in the case of a workman deep inside a hole dug in a cemetery. Again, we're being asked to make sense of a cinematic puzzle (even the village is like a maze); to participate in the film-making process.

And what's the film about? In part, the poetry of life and death: characters quote poets – notably Forough and Omar Khayyam – over and over as they contemplate the pain and pleasures of the here and now, as opposed to the uncertain advantages of the hereafter. But it's also about how city people – media types – come to make films about country people, and how they're often too concerned by their own agenda to pay proper attention to their hosts. The 'director' eventually comes to a glimmer of understanding of how life and death are inextricably entwined (rather than of their suitability for a television scoop), but only after he joins the villagers in saving the unseen hole-digger from a near-fatal accident. But by then, the old lady who'd held out so long is dead …

More life-lessons: the Kiarostami surrogate – a fake engineer – is taught the realities of a woman's lot by a waitress at a (fake) café, in *The Wind Will Carry Us*

5 Kiarostami and Digital: *ABC Africa*

I've dealt with Kiarostami's career at length in order to illustrate how each film develops on the themes, motifs and stylistic tropes of its predecessors. For that reason I'd now like to look at *10*'s immediate predecessor, which some have dismissed as a minor addition to his oeuvre. One can understand how such a view might arise. First, *ABC Africa* – unlike all but a few of his shorts[34] – was a commission, and may be judged less personal in terms of its original inspiration than most of his work. Second, as a documentary-cum-video-diary, it's inevitably seen as less 'creative' than a fiction (though we should be wary of either/or categorisations in the case of Kiarostami). And third, the fact that it was made using digital technology would seem to relegate it, for some, to a kind of second-division film-making. We should not be surprised, however, that Kiarostami followed two major prize-winning films with something unexpected and in many respects rather different. Moreover, I'd argue that the film is actually far more of 'a Kiarostami film' than has been recognised, that it occupies an important place in his career, and that it foreshadows *10* in several respects.

As we see from the opening shot of a letter emerging from a fax machine, the film was made in response to a request from the United Nations' International Fund of Agricultural Development that Kiarostami make a film publicising the work of the Uganda Women's Efforts to Save Orphans programme. The fax itself sets the scene, explaining that due to AIDS and civil war, there are now (this was March 2000) over 1½ million children in Uganda who've lost one or both of their parents. The film then goes on to show Kiarostami and his friend/assistant Seifollah Samadian travelling around Uganda; staying in luxury hotels, they're driven to towns and villages where officials and carers talk about the problems faced and work done by the UWESO project, but where mostly the Iranians just follow and film the children, who clearly enjoy posing, dancing, singing, smiling and playing up for the visitors' cameras. Despite the hardships described, and the material poverty of the environment, we see no suffering until half an hour has passed, when the two men are taken to an AIDS centre.

First we see a coffin-maker's, and then, as we enter the hospital, we hear, for the first time, a child crying. The sound gets louder as the men are led through the wards, and we see children, emaciated and in pain, on the floor and in bed. As we try to adjust to the misery newly on view, we

The cameraman: Kiarostami is
filmed filming for *ABC Africa*

suddenly hear laughter, and then see a doctor and nurse share a joke.
Samadian's camera follows Kiarostami along a corridor; passing a door, he
stops, and the camera follows his gaze to a small body wrapped in cloth,
which a nurse places on a torn-up cardboard box. A makeshift coffin is
made, and the corpse carried to a waiting bicycle, on which it's
precariously balanced and wheeled away – to the rising sound of children
in song; a cut introduces a sea of kids in bright yellow uniforms, and young
women dancing.

This entire sequence lasts five minutes, and is the only time we're
shown the kind of images one would expect in such a film; even then, the
Iranians don't let their cameras linger on any individual's suffering. The
music, colours and laughter again show that 'life goes on'; Kiarostami,
speaking of the vitality and beauty he found in Uganda, has pointed out
that if one person in ten has died due to AIDS or war, we should not
forget that nine out of ten are still alive. Like his previous four features,
this film is not about death but life-and-death: how they're linked, and
what attitude we might adopt with regard to their symbiotic inevitability.

Jonathan Rosenbaum has argued that the film recapitulates aspects of
The Wind Will Carry Us: 'Both films concern – and interrogate, from an
ethical perspective – the position of media people from the city arriving in
a remote and impoverished village to wait for villagers to die.'[35] I'd take
issue with the notion of Kiarostami waiting for people to die – the
discretion of the visuals reflects his feeling that it's pornographic to show
too much of whatever doesn't need to be shown (which here includes
death and suffering, as long as we're aware of their presence) – but
Rosenbaum is right to examine the film in context. He might also have
mentioned *And Life Goes On …*, in which a film-maker visits a region

trying to make sense of the widespread suffering there, and finds the 'victims' more concerned with routine things like watching football than with feeling sorry for themselves.

One scene in *ABC Africa*, especially, echoes that film. In *As Life Goes On ...,* the director stops off at a ruined village, where an old man jokes that even after thousands of innocents have died, people still need functioning toilets, and a woman, in response to the director's son asking how God could let such a catastrophe occur, simply continues with her laundry, shouting at her own child as a lamp is knocked over, 'First the earthquake, then you!' Such pragmatism is again movingly evident in *ABC Africa* when Kiarostami visits a war-torn, windowless house shared by several families; there, he finds that a widower who has lost several children is preparing to marry, that evening, a widow who has also lost several kids. Mehrnaz Saeed-Vafa has written of the use of ruined buildings in both Persian poetry and Iranian cinema as a metaphor for despair,[36] but Kiarostami turns this on its head. This may be a documentary, but even in the most desperate circumstances he still finds room for hope.

The scene immediately preceding this is the film's philosophical core, and reveals how close this documentary is to Kiarostami's fiction. He and Samadian are at their hotel, after their visit to the hospital; the scene opens on mosquitoes buzzing around a lamp, and we hear the men – off-screen, as often – wondering if they carry malaria, which prompts Kiarostami to observe that to die from an insect bite would be the ultimate betrayal; at least with AIDS, somebody somewhere along the line has made some kind of choice. The electricity is suddenly turned off for the night, and as we watch a black screen we hear the men fumbling their way

And life goes on: the director finds love among the ruins in *ABC Africa*

to their rooms, wondering how people who spend so much of their lives in darkness manage – at which Kiarostami notes that, while they themselves are having problems after just five minutes, the remarkable thing about humans is that they can adapt to anything (catastrophes included, we presume). One of the men – we can't tell who – enters his room and settles down to the rumble of an approaching storm. Suddenly a lightning flash illuminates the screen and, for a split second, a silhouette of a tree is framed in a window; as thunder crashes and rain pours, we see it a few more times before the rather swift (since digitally speeded-up) arrival of daylight.

It's not just the fast dawn that suggests this scene may not be 'documentary' at all; is it sheer coincidence that whoever was in the room left a camera turned on towards a window in such a way that, when the lightning comes, it records a perfectly framed tree (a favourite Kiarostami symbol)?[37] The use of darkness – recalling the end of *The Taste of Cherry* – is illuminating: the absence of light makes us think of the sun's importance to the Ugandan villages, so different from our own cosseted homes, as a source of energy, sustenance, life and hope. (Light and darkness are also fundamental to cinema, of course, though Kiarostami wisely doesn't push that point here.) The scene is pivotal; until the hospital visit which preceded it, the film (apart from the interviews with UWESO people) was rather like what any tourist might record – ordinary people going about their lives – but then the shocking sight of suffering and death provokes a more poetic, questioning attitude.

What remains of this partly 'false' documentary, about strong women, vulnerable children and the struggle against death, is charged both by our memories of the hospital and by our awareness that even in times of darkness, there is a prospect of light returning. In one typical Kiarostami shot, a small girl succeeds (in the face of mocking laughter from other kids) in picking up a huge bundle of reeds she's dropped; women and kids listen, laugh and dance en masse to some wonderfully energetic music; and a young couple take an adopted baby on a plane back to Austria and 'a better life'. As the film ends on shots of clouds, with the barely visible faces of children superimposed, we cannot avoid asking ourselves what that 'better life' might be.

6 *10*

(i) Genesis

What is perhaps most remarkable about *ABC Africa* is that such a film –
not only a complex, intelligent reponse to the commission in question, but
one in harmony with the rest of Kiarostami's work – was assembled using
footage originally shot only for research purposes; Kiarostami and
Samadian took digital cameras to Uganda with the idea of using them like
notebooks, and only when they returned to Iran did Kiarostami decide
there was no need to shoot further footage:

I'd already used video at the end of *The Taste of Cherry* after some film I'd
shot was damaged in the lab; I couldn't wait a year for spring to come
round again for a re-shoot, so I used some material shot with my son's
handicam. The people in that footage looked so comfortable in the
camera's presence. Then on *ABC Africa* we were going to use the footage
shot on our research trip to plan our film, but again we felt everyone had
been so relaxed around these little cameras, we could never go back and
make a film that would have been that intimate. So we used that footage
for our film.[38]

Making *ABC Africa* convinced Kiarostami that digital cameras would
allow him to get far more relaxed, naturalistic performances out of his
(non-professional) actors – partly because they are small, partly because
no crew is needed. But there are other benefits:

It frees you up if you want a shot to go on, so you no longer have to *think* in
terms of shots lasting no more than about four minutes or so. It's also freer
in terms of financing and censorship. Then there's the issue of storytelling.
With 35mm there's an expectation for you to tell a story. But with digital, I
think we'll get used to new styles [of film-making], so maybe we need not
rely so much on stories.[39]

Digital seemed the perfect technology – indeed, a *sine qua non* –
for a film he'd been thinking about. A friend had given him the idea
for a film about a psychoanalyst whose office is closed down by the
authorities after a client complains therapy convinced her to sue for
divorce, a move she now regrets; accordingly, the analyst now has to
see clients in her car.

I liked the idea of the car because people talk more easily in cars – plus it's easier for people to watch people talking in cars, because while the camera may be static, it's also mobile because of the car. The car was central, and I didn't want to lose it; the same was true of the idea of using just two camera angles – I wanted to see if it was possible to make a film that way. I wanted it to be a special experience.[40]

While editing *ABC Africa*, Kiarostami began his lengthy preparations for the new film by meeting with many women for five-minute sessions in which he'd ask them to talk to camera about their lives (and particularly about any problems pertinent to being a woman), with a view to casting them as the analyst's clients. But two things changed his mind about the direction the film would take. One was the realisation that, since analysts don't really speak in therapy sessions, any such film would border on a monologue. The other was Mania Akbari, a fan of his work who wrote to Kiarostami offering her services before or behind the camera as soon as she heard he was making a film about women. She describes their initial meeting:

I didn't learn much about the film; he only wanted me to talk about my life and opinions: whether I was a feminist, how I perceived women's roles, their difficulties, their strengths. He was surprised when he discovered I'd had three or four years of therapy, and asked how old I was; I was twenty-seven, but he felt my experiences were like those of an older, more mature woman. The reality was, I was a mother with a ten-year-old son.[41]

From Kiarostami's perspective,

At first Mania thought I was looking for an actor and behaved a bit like a star. She'd misunderstood me, so I told her to be herself. She left and came back the next week with a video cassette, and she was excellent. That's when I found she could become the main character. And I told her that if she wanted, she could introduce me to some people she knew well who could perhaps be in the film; that way, there was no need to build up new relationships for the film.

Akbari agreed. Members of her family – most notably her son Amin – and friends appear in the finished film; her husband also worked on it as an assistant to Kiarostami. The car was Akbari's, like the clothes she wore. The shoot itself, which lasted around three months, was extraordinarily informal and improvisational.

Kiarostami and Mania
Akbari preparing to film
a scene for *10*

We'd shoot two or three days a week. The cameras were at the ready, and I'd be sitting at home with little to do except wait by the phone, so whenever Mania called to say she and her son or friends were available, we'd go out and shoot. We'd film for one or two hours, then go home and check the rushes. If they weren't okay, we'd go out again.[42]

Essentially, as we shall see, the film is a series of conversations. Kiarostami placed two cameras at the front of the car, one trained on the driver's seat, the other on the passenger's. Though it's difficult to gauge precisely how he 'directed' his non-professional cast, what we see clearly had some basis in reality; Kiarostami wanted them to be in the right emotional state in order to bring naturalism to their discussion of particular subjects. Nevertheless, the finished film should not be considered a documentary. Akbari explains how scenes came about:

I never really knew how the film would develop. I just did what was asked of me. Sometimes Kiarostami would tell me precisely what he wanted me to say; often he wouldn't. Sometimes after shooting he'd tell me he hadn't liked me doing certain things; other times he'd be happy and we'd move on. For the film's first sequence, all he really told me was that my character was a mother who'd got divorced – which I was – but then for later sequences he'd include stuff from an earlier script. He never told me what he'd discussed with my son and never told him what he'd discussed with me. He wanted to create surprises.

Though it's based partly on my own experiences, I don't really recognise myself. If I were very close to that character, I'd probably have committed suicide; she's very tough, quite possessive, and lacks calmness – she's slightly lost, like the car. So there's a distance between us. That said, if she weren't a little like me, I wouldn't have been able to play her. So maybe we share quite a lot.[43]

The film was shot more or less in sequence, sometimes with Kiarostami in the back of the car, but more often not.

And I wasn't with them for the important emotional scenes. I'd follow in another car then check the acting on the video, because I believe that when two people talk in a car, they're much more sincere and much closer than they'd be with a third person present – especially if that person's the director!

So while it's difficult if a scene's going the wrong way, if I wait a bit they may come up with something better than I'd have been able to think up. So generally I tried not to be in the car. I was more like an editor than a director, as I wasn't giving directions during shooting;[44] I just made sure they finished with the right sentence at the right time.[45]

Inevitably, like most improvisational methods, this approach not only meant that a huge amount of work was done both pre- and post-filming, but made for a high shooting ratio – a far less costly problem, of course, with digital. Kiarostami ended up with almost twenty-three hours' footage, and four or five more characters than appeared in the finished film, which he cut to run a little over one and a half hours. 'I could've made maybe ten other films from the material we had. But in the end you have to choose.'

The film was finished. For Kiarostami it had been an experiment; he'd asked Akbari not to tell anyone about the film, and her son Amin didn't

In the Cannes: Kiarostami and Mania Akbari at the premiere of *10*

even believe they'd really made one – where had the crew and actors been? Kiarostami was unsure people would be able to stand ninety minutes in one car. 'But when I showed it to friends I had good reactions, and then Marin Karmitz wanted it to play in Cannes. Last night it did, and people seemed to like it. So I realised we'd done it.'[46]

(ii) The Narrative

With the exception of a single shot, *10* is set entirely within the confines of a car being driven around the streets of Tehran, and shot using just two angles, with the camera or cameras situated roughly in the middle of the dashboard and directed either at the driver's or the passenger's seat, regardless of who's speaking at any given moment. There is no discernible camera movement.[47]

The narrative is divided into ten chapters or segments, each comprising a different dialogue. They are prefaced, respectively, by the numbers ten to one, in graphics reminiscent of the countdown figures on film leader; as each number appears it is accompanied by a whirring sound evocative of a film projector, followed by the ring of a bell like that heard at the start or end of a round in boxing or wrestling.[48]

10. Amin, a boy of ten, climbs into the car to be driven to the swimming pool by his mother, Mania.[49] He complains that she's late, and an argument quickly develops in which the boy voices his anger at his mother for having divorced his father and his dislike for his new stepfather. He accuses her of selfishness, while she tries to quieten him and explain her actions. His tantrum continues, however, and as soon as they're in the vicinity of the pool, he storms from the car, leaving his mother – whom

Back to basics: the chapter headings

we now, after about fifteen minutes, see for the very first time – drained by the exchange and testily trying to park.

9. A woman sits in the passenger seat, evidently alone and unself-consciously picking at facial spots. Eventually, a cut announces the arrival of Mania; the passenger is apparently her sister, and as Mania drives her home, they discuss birthdays, Amin's moodiness whenever he visits their mother, and whether he should be allowed yet to go and live full-time with Mania's ex-husband.

8. Mania gives a lift to an old woman who visits a local shrine three times a day. The woman talks about having rid herself of most of her possessions since her husband's death, and tries, without success, to persuade Mania to go and pray while she looks after the car.

7. It's night; a prostitute has climbed by mistake into Mania's car when she braked, and Mania, curious, asks about the woman's work and her attitude to love and sex. The prostitute, unrepentant about enjoying her job, argues that she does the same as wives do: she's just smarter and more honest about it. When she leaves the car, the film's one change of camera angle occurs; looking forwards from the car, we watch her walk to an intersection where she's at once approached by a kerb-crawler. We see her rejecting the offer, but she then gets into another car that stops just seconds later.

6. Leaving the shrine, Mania gives a lift to a young woman she's noticed there. Mania admits she never thought she'd take up prayer, but it sometimes assuages feelings of guilt. Her passenger, meanwhile, hopes it might make her boyfriend less hesitant to marry.

5. Mania collects Amin from his father to take him to his grandmother's, but the boy, who is moody and a little feverish, soon starts arguing about the route she takes. As they discuss which cartoons he likes, he lets drop that his dad (with whom he now lives) watches 'sexy' programmes on television late at night.

4. It's night again; Mania collects a friend to take her out to dinner, but she sobs throughout the journey, distraught that her husband has left her. Mania reminds her there are other fish in the sea, tells her she must learn to love herself, and rebukes her for letting her happiness depend on the whims of one man.

3. Amin, in a slightly better mood than previously, demands to be driven to his grandmother's, and Mania jokes with him about getting his father to marry someone who has a daughter suitable for himself; this leads to an initially good-humoured discussion of what makes a good wife – evidently not someone like Mania, given that Amin again starts

complaining that she always prioritised her needs over those of himself and his father.

2. Mania gives a lift to her friend from the shrine, who is upset that her boyfriend has ended their relationship; she knows, however, that time heals and admits she's sad just because she misses him. When the woman's scarf slips to reveal that she's cropped her hair, Mania encourages her to remove it altogether, and while wiping a tear from her friend's cheek, compliments her on her beauty, courage and sensible attitude.

1. Mania collects Amin from her ex-husband. When he immediately announces that he wants to be taken to his grandma's, she simply says 'All right', and drives off. The image fades to black and the closing credits roll, as a piano plays Howard Blake's 'Walking in the Air'.

Given, on the one hand, the constraints Kiarostami imposed upon himself (the single setting, the camera angles) and, on the other, the potential for chaos of his unusual approach to 'direction', *10*'s narrative is remarkable in being at once rich *and* coherent. Breaking it down into ten chapters was clearly useful in that it allowed him to create, from little more than dialogue, a number of discrete narrative building blocks that make sense in themselves while offering opportunities for further enrichment in terms of how they might interact with one another. This peculiar combination of rigour and freedom gives the film a distinctive Kiarostami quality, whereby it seems almost as if the narrative is organically growing before our very eyes; for quite a while there doesn't even seem to be any 'story' at all.

Because Kiarostami prefers us to interact with a film by working on what we see and hear with our imaginations; because he is therefore happy to tell us only as much as we absolutely need to know and no more; because his 'actors' are therefore behaving as they would in real life, without ever feeling the need to keep us clued in to every carefully worked-out detail of what is happening[50] – because of all this, the film gives an unusually strong impression of being 'real' in terms of what it depicts. The arguments, for instance, between mother and son have a searing intensity virtually unprecedented in the cinema, partly, of course, because they are taking place between a real mother and son and are inspired to some extent by real feelings,[51] but also partly because Kiarostami has as far as possible removed the conventional cinematic apparatus from the equation. Just as there is no camera crew, no on-set director and no professional actors, so there is no script forcing the actors to say or do the kind of things that get said or done in worked-through fictions. The result is an almost documentary-like verisimilitude that at times attains an emotional power quite amazing in a film that appears so utterly dependent on conversation. [52]

That said, Kiarostami is not known for conventional dramatic climaxes, and for a film so evocative of ordinary, everyday existence, he was unlikely to change his ways in this regard. If there is a 'climax', it comes when Mania's friend's scarf slips to reveal her closely cropped hair, and continues through the moment when Mania wipes a tear from her cheek. (This is the most conspicuous example of the very few occasions in the film when a hand of the person not being shown by the camera at that moment slips into the frame.[53]) In conventional dramaturgical terms, this is an unusually quiet moment for an emotional climax, but it is perhaps characteristic of Kiarostami in that it involves a kind of epiphany. It is also significant that it comes in the penultimate chapter of the film, rather than at the very end, in that it allows the very short final chapter to provide one of the director's customarily ambiguous or 'open' endings. In (1), nothing has changed – the boy still insists peremptorily on being taken to his grandmother's, and his mother still acquiesces – except Mania's attitude. Her 'all right' (spoken while she's off-screen) is very different to the stridently frustrated voice we heard off-screen in (10); she has been on a journey, and through her experiences has found for herself a level of calm perfectly expressed by the closing music.

(iii) The Boy

Though the film's 'climax' comes in its ninth chapter (2), there is no denying that the most emotional intensity is to be found in the extraordinary argument between Mania and Amin that takes up most of the first chapter (10). Lasting around eighteen minutes, this is by far the longest chapter, and crucial in that it introduces various basic problems relevant to what follows: Amin is upset that his mother divorced his father, and dislikes living with her and her new husband Morteza. He considers her selfish, and expresses disgust at her having accused his father of addiction to drugs in order to get a divorce. He repeatedly accuses her of never listening to him, and calls her a stupid cow who'll never amount to anything.

It's very intriguing that Kiarostami chose to begin the film the way he did. While it's clearly important to impart information to the audience, it's strange that he chose to show, for the entirety of the film's first sixteen minutes, only the boy. Even if he had not been famous for having made films about children in a world controlled by adults, this opening

'Quite enough masculinity for the whole film': Amin lays down the law

would still have given the impression that Amin was to be the central character in the film – an impression which, of course, turns out to be false. So why choose this strategy?

'Actually, it wasn't possible to cut it any other way, because the boy's actions were not as good as his *reactions* to what Mania was saying. So I had to keep showing him listening to her.'[54]

Even so, it is unusually extreme not to show her at all, especially since the opening shot of Amin is not, despite appearances to the contrary, a single continuous take; indeed, by this writer's estimate there are around thirteen jump cuts, almost but not quite invisible. These, Kiarostami insists, are not the result of the boy having performed poorly.

He was almost never wrong. Sometimes the light was bad, things became too impolite, or someone outside would spot the camera and give the V-sign or come to the window and ask what we were doing. But most people don't notice the cuts anyway, because we kept the sound and dialogue continuous. They're not important cuts, after all.[55]

And they did enable him to assemble an argument whose duration and dynamics are absolutely plausible; the quarrel's pauses and digressions, depressions and crescendos are like a carefully orchestrated concerto of regret, recrimination and revenge. But this doesn't explain precisely why Kiarostami felt it necessary to give the impression of a single take and let us see only the boy.

If I didn't show Mania's face, I felt that any mother in the audience would be able to understand her; they wouldn't judge her by her appearance. I really don't want viewers to judge my characters, which is why sometimes I don't show them at all. Just hearing them can be enough.[56]

That said, we do see and hear the boy, and it's impossible – even with the strident voice off-screen – not to feel, watching this sequence, that he's at the very least 'difficult'. If he is to be the central character, it's unlikely we'll be able to identify with him easily. But we already know that from other Kiarostami films. True, we'd all like to think we're as altruistic as the young hero of *Where Is the Friend's House?*, but Kiarostami provides few figures we actively admire and want to imitate. Amin is not so different from the kids in *The Traveller*, *Homework* or *And Life Goes On …*, in that his main concern in life is sport and cartoons, except that he has a parental divorce to deal with as well, which is making his enjoyment of those things more difficult. He blames his mother for that, and we hear her accuse him, in (10), of parroting whatever his father says about her. She's probably right: Amin's most notable characteristic is that he's an archetypal chauvinist male in miniature. In (3), when mother and son joke about what makes an ideal wife, it becomes clear that for him intelligence, independence and a loving nature are unimportant; what matters is that the woman should be obedient, stay at home, cook, clean and cater to the needs of the men in her family. Amin, in fact, is not only a child but the embodiment of masculine arrogance and power in a film devoid of speaking parts for adult men.[57] As Akbari has said, 'He represented quite enough masculinity for the whole film.'[58] (And we should not forget, of course, the Freudian resonance of his invective against his mother's new partner – a resonance which is appropriate not only to the film's subject matter but also to its origins as a project about a psychoanalyst.)

It's interesting to learn how Kiarostami engineered chapter (3).

It came from real life. I had a good relationship with Mania and her husband; I knew about their lives and could build on that. So I reminded Amin of what he'd thought some time earlier, and told him to say something along those lines. So the idea was mine but the dialogue belongs to the actor. I need to know the actor so that everything can come from their character, but then I take that, work on it and give it back to them.[59]

(iv) The Driver

We first see the driver, Mania, sixteen minutes into the film, after her son has stormed from the car calling her a stupid idiot. We may be surprised by what we see. Despite the very evident strain and fatigue on her face, she looks much younger than we imagined from her raised voice and hectoring words; she's also beautiful and sophisticated-looking, well dressed and made-up, with smart sunglasses. We haven't seen anyone like this in Kiarostami's films before. Indeed, we probably haven't seen anyone like this in any Iranian movie.

What we discover, as the film progresses, is that this woman is also intelligent, articulate, feisty and very independent. In her arguments with her son, Mania not only argues that she had to divorce her first husband because she was stifled by the marriage, but defends her dishonesty to the court – claiming he was a drug addict – on the grounds that it was her only way out: 'The rotten laws of this society give no rights to women.' She is concerned about her son's welfare and development, but is not about to sacrifice her life to his unreasonable demands; she may not have devoted much time to cooking, but that's because she finds photography and painting more fulfilling.[60] She is sufficiently open-minded and curious about life to give a lift to a prostitute and ask about her work, but also sensitive enough to take the advice of a pious old woman and try prayer as a means of bringing some tranquillity into her life. (Incidentally, in the film this development comes immediately after, and may be a consequence of, the prostitute's assertion that all married women are in fact selling themselves to men – and probably deluding themselves, into the bargain, about their husbands' fidelity.) And when a friend sinks into pathetically self-piteous sobbing at her husband having left her, Mania takes her to task, castigating her clinging, dependent ways and quoting a 'bitch' at a local health club as saying: 'Women need a big ass or big tits – that's what men like.'[61]

Amin's mother revealed …

This, then, is the person who takes over from Amin as the central character in the film. Like most Kiarostami protagonists, she remains, finally, too much of a mystery to function fully as an identification figure, but she's certainly a very plausible, rounded character, and we're likely to feel pleased by her newly found calmness at the end of the film. By then we've been on a journey with her; like the boy in *Where Is the Friend's House?* and the directors in *And Life Goes On …* and *The Wind Will Carry Us*, she has learnt from her encounters and, apparently, put those lessons to use, even though her journey is far from over:

The journey is very important to me. It's like all my roads: you don't know how far they go, there are no signs telling you where they lead and you don't know where they end. But it's important just to be moving …[62]

For *10*, Kiarostami had himself taken a journey into uncharted territory, since this was his first film with a female protagonist. Indeed, the fact that he'd never focused on female experience before had been seen by some as a failing,[63] though as Mehrnaz Saeed-Vafa points out in discussing the shortage of women in his work, 'what is interesting is that often in his films, absences strongly suggest presences'.[64] And in 1999, when asked why he hadn't shown more women in his films, Kiarostami gave the following response:

Frankly, I think my perspective on Iranian women is completely at variance with what you see in contemporary Iranian films. In those I've seen, I can divide the women into two or three types: the woman who is merely a mother figure and no more; the lover figure – who was more conspicuous in the pre-Revolutionary films, but who's still there as long as an excuse can be found for including her (this applies to second-wife roles, too); and the victim who has been beaten up and suffered a great deal. And then there are the historical examples from mythology. But I don't like these types. And I know there are exceptional women around, but I don't like to deal with exceptional cases either. And sometimes invisibility can be quite telling, anyway – think of *The Taste of Cherry*.[65]

In fact, from *The Traveller* onwards we often see strong, working mothers (albeit mostly as background figures); in *Through the Olive Trees*, the director's assistant is a very competent professional woman; *The Wind Will Carry Us* not only has the director repeatedly taking calls on a mobile phone from a female boss in Tehran, but includes a wonderfully funny scene in which the proprietress of the village café takes him to task by reminding him that women never stop waiting upon idle men, even at night; and *ABC Africa* is in part a tribute to the determination, strength and selflessness of Uganda's women. To some extent, moreover, Kiarostami's hands were tied by the strict codes of Islamic practice surrounding the making of films and what was allowed to be depicted in them; because they might have necessitated showing things that would not have occurred in real life, the restrictions described in chapter 3 (see p. 18) may have put him off the idea of making films with major roles for women. At any rate, whatever the reason, with *10* he made up for lost time.

(v) The Passengers

With the sole exception of her son (who appears in four chapters), all Mania's passengers are women: her married sister, who accompanies her when she goes to buy her husband a birthday cake; an old woman walking to a shrine to whom she gives a lift; a young prostitute she quizzes about her work; a woman of roughly her own age whom she meets when she starts visiting the shrine herself, and to whom she gives a second lift in the penultimate chapter; and a friend distraught at the fact that her husband of seven years has left her. In age, experience and attitude, these characters are notable for their diversity. It's surely no accident, for example, that the chapter with the old woman whose piety suggests she 'represents' the sacred occurs in daylight and is followed by a night sequence with the (presumably teenage[66]) prostitute, whose language and approach to life could not be more profane; nor that the pathetic weeping of Mania's abandoned friend (again filmed at night, and covering her face with her hand) contrasts with the behaviour of the next woman we see, calmly and bravely discussing the loss of her own fiancé as, in broad daylight, she removes her scarf to (in Mania's words) let her head breathe.

Of recent Iranian films dealing with the plight of women, several have presented a cross-section of female characters; the best known to have played abroad include Tahmineh Milani's *Two Women* (*Do zan*, 1999), Marziyeh Meshkini's *The Day I Became a Woman* (*Rooze keh zan shodam*, 2000), Panahi's *The Circle* and Mehrjui's *Stay Alive* (*Bemani*, 2002). *The Circle* apart, some of these films are, for all their many virtues, a little schematic in their characterisations; indeed, Milani's film verges on the stereotypical in its use of simplistic polarities. It is appropriate, then, to consider whether the passengers in *10* are mere ciphers illustrating different aspects of female experience, or are sufficiently well drawn to convince us they exist as proper individuals.

Akbari has praised the film's accuracy while admitting it might also be interpreted on a metaphorical level.

It's certainly a more authentic picture of women in Tehran. It shows women who are or want to be independent; women still attached – perhaps too attached – to a man; and shows some people are prepared to speak up for themselves. But it's also true that they might all be one woman, that they might reflect the different parts of one woman's mind. The mother, the lover, the rebel, a woman in grief ... all these could reflect aspects of one woman's life.[67]

Indeed, for its Cannes premiere, *10* was described in the following words (presumably provided by or used with the permission of Kiarostami): 'ten sequences in the emotional lives of six women and the challenges that they face at one particular moment of the lives, that could just as easily be ten sequences in the emotional life of the one same women ...'[68]

Such an approach could lead to stereotyping, but Kiarostami's methods keep the characterisations firmly within the realm of plausibility. That is partly a matter of having non-professional actors 'play' themselves – characters and dialogue are closely derived from reality. But it is also a matter of how the film was shot and edited. Using a digital camera meant there were no crew and (most of the time) no director to make the cast self-conscious; Akbari has spoken of how easy it was to forget there was a camera in the car.[69] Then there is the fact that Kiarostami often leaves in the film what other film-makers might remove. For example, at the start of chapter (9) – which *in toto* lasts around twelve minutes – two minutes pass before there's any dialogue at all, during which time we see a woman (we have no idea yet who she is; only with Mania's return to the car will we find out she's her sister) distractedly picking at a facial spot and fanning herself as she watches the world outside the car – a world, incidentally, which we cannot see for ourselves, since the light is so bright everything beyond the window is bleached white. There's no 'story' here, and almost no information, other than that it's hot and the woman is uncomfortable in her heavy *chador*. Even so, Kiarostami repeats the strategy later in the same chapter, when Mania goes into a bakery for a minute or so. Such 'dead moments' enhance the impression of documentary authenticity, and make us believe in the woman as more than just a character type:

I didn't ask her to scratch her face. Sometimes when I see my old films, I find I like most the bits that weren't really directed; accidents are often more

All uphill from here? *And Life Goes On...*

The end of the road? *The Taste of Cherry*

The single tree? There are so many.

Where next? *The Wind Will Carry Us*

A woman's lot? *ABC Africa*

A half-life?

Where next?

In need of fresh air?

In need of spiritual succour?

Want me to drop you off?

In need of money or men?

What's out there?

Is it really so terrible?

Is there an alternative?

Breaking the frame?

Breaking the law?

Breaking the illusion?:
A Taste of Cherry

Who's there? *The Wind Will Carry Us*

What's out there in the darkness? *ABC Africa*

What's beneath our very feet? *10 on Ten* (MK2 Production, 2004)

Distant: *Five* (MK2
Productions, 2004)

Stray dog: *Five*

Drifting clouds: *Five*

Reflected...

Hidden...

Reassessed...

Photographs by Abbas Kiarostami, *Photographies, Photographs, Fotografie* (Éditions Hazan, 1999)

A 'dead moment': Mania's sister simply observed

important to your work than what's intended. Something happens by chance that's close to your subject … There are basically two kinds of storytelling. One's direct, very eventful, like a serial. The other's about looking at something and finding something in it for yourself. This woman presented herself as very fortunate: married, a daughter, in control. That's what she gave off. But when the camera stayed on her, while Mania went to buy something, you found something a little different: not a story, but something more …[70]

Kiarostami forestalls any reading of his characters merely as types in other subtle ways. The old woman (shown in daylight) is followed, in the narrative, by the prostitute (picked up at night); if that were merely a contrast, the film would be guilty of simplistic schematism. But Kiarostami slyly and repeatedly blurs any lines that would pigeon-hole and separate the women.

That we never *see* the prostitute in the passenger seat not only implies that she's a real streetwalker but links her to the old woman, glimpsed only momentarily as she enters and leaves the car; are we being gently reminded that what they have in common is more important than what divides them? After all, Mania's abandoned friend, who believes in loving one man alone, is also filmed at night, which links her with the prostitute who, we may remember, admitted to having once been overly dependent on a man who let her down. Moreover, the words Mania uses to try to give this woman strength echo those she heard used by the prostitute. Hence, chapter (4) functions in various ways: as a portrait of a recently abandoned woman which reflects back to the prostitute's past and forwards to what might befall Mania's friend if she can't overcome her immature dependence on men; as another step in Mania's own growing self-confidence and self-awareness; as another tale of male selfishness and unreliability; and as a contrast to the behaviour of another woman who has been abandoned, and whose unveiling will come to serve, as stated previously, as the film's emotional climax.

But why, precisely, is this woman's removal of her veil so moving? Partly, of course, because her shorn head is evidence of her grief and anger at her ex-fiancé's decision not to marry but to finish with her; in such situations, people often cut their hair as a symbolic act of starting anew. This, coupled with words to the effect that she knows she'll get over her unhappiness, is evidence not only of her suffering but of her strength. But it's also something of a revelation; as Mania says, the woman does look beautiful – rather more than we could have imagined – with her head bare and her hair so short.[71]

Most importantly, it's an expression of personal freedom, of independence in a male-dominated world. Hamid Naficy has described how veiling is not purely a matter of restriction, but 'a dynamic practice in which both men and women are implicated', which allows women 'a great deal of latitude in how they present themselves to the gaze of the male onlookers'.[72] In terms of cinematic representation, however, and certainly within the context of the world created in 10, veiling is undoubtedly restrictive. It is not permissible for women to appear unveiled in Iranian films; moreover, within 10, with its emblematic mini-chauvinist and its protagonist complaining about 'the rotten laws of this society' and fickle, stifling men, the veil may be seen as a symbol of the oppression women face in contemporary Iran.[73] The character, the actor and the film itself

The 'dramatic climax':
Mania's friend unexpectedly
unveiled

are all in transgression of the Islamic Republic's codes;[74] and what makes the act still more affecting is the way it is gently encouraged and applauded by Mania, whose hand enters twice from the right-hand side of the frame to wipe a tear from her friend's cheek, in a simple, understated, profoundly eloquent display of sisterhood. Till then, the film's idiosyncratic visual strategy has kept the characters separate, locked in compositional boxes; it's as if Kiarostami were telling us that rules – social or self-imposed, cinematic or ideological – can and probably should be broken when human needs and happiness are at stake.

At first I didn't like this [disruption of the frame] much, because I prefer not to show big emotional moments. So I asked them to do the scene again and not do that. But little by little I changed my mind, and finally decided it was okay.[75]

(vi) The Car
One reason the unveiling in chapter (9) is so affecting is that it occurs in broad daylight: the woman's courage is all the more evident in that she is visible to passers-by, in a car stationary at the time. The moment is significant in that it reveals the dual function of a car as a private space which has several characteristics (visibility, the possibility of movement, etc.) often associated with public space – one of several factors, one suspects, that has made the car appealing to Kiarostami.

From *Bread and Alley* onwards, journeys informed much of his work, but it was really only with *And Life Goes On …* that he began to explore the expressive potential of cars: the traffic jams speak of the protagonist's impatience, and the final shot of his car climbing the mountain track reveals his determination. In *The Taste of Cherry* the main character's slow, meandering progress around the hillside roads mirrors the difficulty and delicacy of the task he's set himself, and in *The Wind Will Carry Us* the director explicitly likens himself to his car. To some extent, Kiarostami identifies drivers with their vehicles, and in *10* it's fascinating (especially given the spontaneous way it was made) to see how emotion may be mirrored by the car's motion. When Mania is exhausted after her first argument with Amin, she has problems parking; with the old woman, she drives slowly; when things have improved enough with Amin for them to joke together, she takes a fast ring-road which creates a sense of openness and exhilarating speed (see this book's front cover); and at the film's tenderest, most contemplative moment, when she offers comfort to her new friend, she has parked the car in what appears to be a quiet back street.

Kiarostami, who famously enjoys the privacy and freedom afforded by driving, has given several reasons as to why he likes to shoot scenes set in cars. In *10 on Ten* (2004), a fascinating masterclass film made for workshop students which also serves as a DVD extra, he argues that because people sit side by side, only making eye contact when they feel like it, they speak more freely; that traffic helps to create tension or arguments; and that in *10* the enclosed space reflects the protagonist's painful predicament. Certainly, watching the film gives an impression of claustrophobia that's wholly appropriate to talk of stifling marriages, rotten laws and relationships that are unstable and unreliable.

But what's especially intriguing, given the specific circumstances of this being a film about women in Iran, is that the car is at once to some extent an outdoor, public space (insofar as it is not the private space of a home, which Kiarostami would legally be unable to film with any honesty or accuracy) *and* an enclosed, private space where intimate conversations may take place. Moreover, in this film, many of the conversations centre on what occurs in private homes; we may see and hear people inside the car, but we learn mainly about what happens behind closed doors – in Mania's past and present homes, at the saint's shrine, in the places the prostitute visits with her clients, etc. etc.[76] Moreover, we hear about men: about Amin's father watching porn late at night; about husbands called by wives on their mobiles replying that they're stuck at work when in fact they're with a whore; about husbands and boyfriends leaving wives and fiancées; about dead husbands and sons (in the case of the pious old

From a car window: Amin temporarily leaving the custody of his father

woman); and about men like Mania's second husband who offer support and companionship.[77] Since the Islamic codes pertaining to cinema prevent so much of what occurs between women and men being depicted in a realistically plausible way, Kiarostami uses the private/public space of the car to engage our imaginations (as well as those of the driver and passengers) about what may be happening elsewhere. In short, a major part of the film actually occupies a realm that is imagined, and invisible.

In a review for the *Village Voice*, J. Hoberman wrote of an unusually independent Iranian woman 'who serves as our Virgil'.[78] The phrase is evocative both in implying that Mania is our guide to a hidden, subterranean domain of suffering which – at least in the film's own terms – is as imaginary as Dante's, and in touching on the importance of journeys and guide-figures in the mystic tradition of Persian poetry.[79] But if Mania is our guide, it is surely also true that, in some respects, her passengers serve as guides for her, leading her, through a combination of advice, example and experience, to a deeper understanding of herself and the world in which she lives.

(vii) The City

The world of *10* is the city of Tehran, a location rather less visually attractive than the mountainous areas seen in most of Kiarostami's road movies. As Stephen Bransford has argued regarding the earlier work,

While we can and should understand Kiarostami's films as road movies, we shouldn't associate his films with the sense of placelessness and blinding speed that is typical of most modern road movies … Vehicles in Kiarostami's films do not function as the means by which drivers and viewers arrive at a final destination, but rather as sophisticated instruments of social and geographical scrutiny.[80]

But *10* differs from the earlier work in certain crucial respects: not only does all the travelling occur in urban areas, but the overall impression left by the ten journeys is one of geographical circularity (as opposed to a somewhat meandering linearity). Moreover, of course, almost without exception the cameras are located inside the car and trained on the people in the front seats, which greatly restricts our view.

So what exactly does the 'social and geographical scrutiny' in *10* reveal in terms of what lies beyond the car windows? Very little, in fact. We do get the impression that the traffic in Tehran can be problematically heavy:

It was impossible for us to control the environment outside the car – people were very interested in what we were up to – so we just made sure we kept to the right as much as possible. Actually, what you see is not really like the traffic in Tehran, which is far worse.[81]

The architecture – shops, apartment blocks, a school, walls around the shrine, freeway bridges and verges – is non-descript. As for people, we see a great many men driving, a traffic cop, a man asking Mania for a tip for helping her at the bakery, a car full of men noisily objecting when she points out they're driving the wrong way in a one-way street, and a couple of army officers standing on the pavement and watching her drive off as she collects Amin at the start of chapters (5) and (1).[82] Mainly men. At one point we see a huddle of three stout women in dark *chadors*, and in chapter (9) Mania offers a lift to an elderly woman whom her sister laughingly describes as being 'on her last legs' – Mania responds she'll be the same one day.[83] Otherwise, female society is represented almost exclusively by the passengers and their driver – a numerical imbalance in the film's visual account of urban life which serves, perhaps, to remind us that men have more freedom in public spaces than women.

(It is perhaps appropriate here to reveal that the woman who regularly visits Ali Akbar's shrine was not even aware she was being filmed.

I'd been looking for an elderly woman to cast for a long while. I saw this woman walking into the shrine each day, and thought she'd have so much to say. So we waited for her – by then I knew her schedule – and she got in the car, talked and got out. I didn't give her anything to say, and she didn't realise what was happening. But she'll never see the film; she doesn't need to.[84]

A man's world: glimpses of Tehran

Take me to grandma's.

Understandably concerned about invading the privacy of someone so devout, Kiarostami chose not to use any footage of her in the passenger's seat.[85])

Kiarostami did tell Akbari which routes to take through the streets of Tehran, but this was

mainly because the light was important. I didn't want to show too much of what was happening outside the car, as I didn't want viewers to become distracted. As it is, expatriate Iranians sometimes come up and ask me about how the city has changed, after recognising an uncle's house or whatever; but obviously I'd rather they focused on the film itself.[86]

But he was clearly optimistic that restricting our view of the city would succeed to some degree, since he created at least one journey that doesn't make proper logical sense. In chapter (9) Mania starts the car and chats with her sister while en route to a bakery; upon arrival, she parks the car in the very spot where their journey began, which means that her sister's instructions ('Park over there – the baker's is just here') were in fact superfluous. (Not unreasonably, Kiarostami hoped and expected most people would inspect the film less closely than the author of this book!)

We do, then, get a strong impression that we're seeing something of Tehran, even though we're not. We *feel* we've witnessed life there because glimpses of people on the streets have been combined with spoken accounts – deceitful or truthful, we cannot say – of life indoors. Image and sound, public and private, documentary and fiction have been very carefully combined by Kiarostami – who, ironically, in a written statement for the Cannes premiere, outlined his efforts to bring about 'the disappearance of direction'.[87]

(viii) The Director: 'directing'
In considering to what extent Kiarostami's films are political, Mehrnaz Saeed-Vafa points out how, in his work, characters are often defined through their jobs; the director himself told her, in February 2000, 'As soon as you have a job you become political.'[88] Such a statement is obviously relevant to the characters in *10*,[89] but it's also relevant to the director himself. How does Kiarostami see his job, as far as *10* is concerned? What is he doing, and why?

We've already noted how the film's minimalist methodology – the two camera angles, characters playing themselves, detailed discussions and

lengthy preparation leading to largely improvised takes, and so on –
constitute an attempt to engage the audience in a more intimate
relationship with reality or truth by abandoning much of the traditional
film-making apparatus. We've also noted how that included reducing, or
modifying, much of what's conventionally regarded as the work of the
director. By absenting himself from so much of the 'shoot' and using pre-
planned dialogue and situations even less than he has in the past,
Kiarostami has to some degree turned himself into a strange hybrid: an
editor of what might even be termed 'found footage' who also happens to
be the film's prime mover, with absolute creative control over how it is
originated, made and completed. In *10 on Ten* he explains how neither
réalisateur nor *metteur en scène* are accurate as terms to describe what he
did for the film: he collaborates closely with non-professional actors in
recording a 'reality' which he created only in its broad outlines; they (and
accidents) provide the details, which he then uses as his basic materials in
post-production.

Politically, this increases the level of collaboration with others, and
diminishes the master–servant dynamic Kiarostami clearly finds distasteful
in professional relationships.[90] His strategy, however, also involves an
attempt to re-think the relationship of the director to the viewer. By
asking, even insisting that the spectator interact with a film, Kiarostami is
adhering to his belief that 'To captivate a viewer is to rob him of his
reason'.[91] And the way he has ensured that the viewer *has* to use his
imagination when watching one of his films is to create ambiguity through
the principles of subtraction and omission.

One finds this strategy at work not only in Kiarostami's preference for
narrative ellipses but in his tendency to keep things hidden or secret;
indeed, he often uses outright deceit as a method, and has often argued to
the effect that it is through lies that one gets to the truth. The most
obvious example of this in *10* is in his filming of chapter (7), with the
prostitute. The fact that almost the entire sequence is shot at night with
the camera for once trained exclusively on Akbari strongly implies that this
is a real prostitute; we see her only when she walks into the distance to be
picked up by a kerb-crawler. In fact, the truth could not have been more
different.

I had many phone conversations with prostitutes, but no one really
impressed me. Not everyone can act well in films, and sometimes fiction is
more realistic than reality. Very often the prostitutes were acting more

respectably than housewives; when I explained what they had to discuss, they'd say, 'I can't do that!'[92]

So he had to write the dialogue and look around for someone else; eventually, the role was played by Akbari's younger sister.

She was twenty-one, and her experience of men was very limited. She was kissed at seventeen and cried for three days; that was it until she married. Then, three or four days after the wedding, her husband had gone to Canada, where she was to join him a little later. So her experience of sexual matters was very limited, but she was quite wonderful in the film. Plus, of course, it helped that Mania felt comfortable with her. But the woman you see walking off along the street was not her but a friend of mine who I asked just to do that shot; the car she gets into was driven by Mania's husband.[93]

This last shot – the only one to break with the two-angle method – was included because Kiarostami 'wanted to show how men there are just waiting in the streets. Two cars come along in a matter of seconds – the first for real! – which looks really predatory.'[94]

Such deceptions have played an important part in Kiarostami's methods for years. It's now known that for *The Taste of Cherry* most of the actors shown talking in the lead character's car never actually met: 'Kiarostami filmed each of them alone, occupying the passenger seat while Ershadi drove and the driver's seat while each of the others was a passenger … he thus performed, or played, all these people off-screen, soliciting on-screen dialogue and reactions.'[95] Unseen characters abound in *Where Is the Friend's House?* and the other Koker films; key events are not shown (or, indeed, properly heard) in *Close-Up*; over a dozen characters in *The Wind Will Carry Us* are never shown;[96] and the centrality and artifice of *ABC Africa*'s hotel-blackout scene were earlier noted.

Kiarostami makes very telling use of secrets, lies and invisibility, and in *10 on Ten* quotes both Bresson – to the effect that art is created not by addition but by subtraction – and Nietzsche: 'That which is truly deep needs a mask'. It is all part of making viewers use their imaginations:

When you see Mania asking someone if they want to move out of a parking place, it would be pointless actually to show that person; your imagination helps you to 'see' things that aren't shown. All too often cinema and television show things you can't even see in real life: open-heart surgery, for example. Showing too much of what it's not necessary to show … to me, it's pornography.[97]

One should, then, perhaps also bear in mind the possible influence on Kiarostami's work of traditional Islamic notions of what's permissible and forbidden (*halal* and *haram*), and of Iranian hermeneutics, based, according to Hamid Naficy, 'on the primacy of hiding the core values (that is, of veiling) and of distrusting manifest meanings (that is, vision)'.[98] Saeed-Vafa aligns this to the importance in Iranian culture of symbolism, metaphor and allegory, especially in poetry; indeed, she argues, 'Because of Iran's traditions and social conditions, Iranian culture and politics demand a covert expression of subject and self.'[99]

(ix) The Director: 'directed'

Many of my films have autobiographical elements – though in *The Taste of Cherry* I don't identify with the character's suicidal sentiments. In my view, if a film-maker can't find a kindred spirit among his characters, he's in danger of being just a narrator, with no real feeling for his characters.'[100]

As long ago as 1980, when his off-screen voice was heard in the short *Orderly or Disorderly*, Kiarostami explicitly registered himself as a cinematic presence influencing the making of that very film. By the end of the decade, with *Homework* (in which we both hear him off-screen and are shown him as a faintly threatening interrogator of the boys who are his subjects) and *Close-Up* (in which he adopts an openly active role in shaping the protagonist's 'story'), Kiarostami was not only making his authorial presence felt – in line with the modernist tradition – but questioning the ethics of his position vis-à-vis his subjects. In *Close-Up*, for example, we hear him tell Sabzian, as he sits in the courtroom, that the camera will help to explain and clarify things; as we've seen, however, it does nothing of the sort – it *increases* our doubts about what we see and hear. Small wonder Sabzian says he'd like to believe that there are directors who care about ordinary people and don't separate themselves from the world.

That issue is central to Kiarostami's subsequent work. The director has no need literally to be heard or seen in the film himself in order to be a perceived presence. We've noted the Kiarostami surrogates – the directors – in *And Life Goes On …*, *Through the Olive Trees* and *The Wind Will Carry Us*, all of whom prompt the viewer to reflect on the purpose of art and,

Branching out: Abbas
Kiarostami in *10 on Ten*

more specifically, on the relationship of the rich city types to the poor
country people they employ in their films.[101] Jonathan Rosenbaum, writing
about the last of these films, argues that 'in comically divvying up his world
between media "experts" and peasants – moguls with cellular phones and
ordinary working people – he's raising the issue of whom this world
actually belongs to, both deservedly and in fact'.[102] But it's crucial to
remember this is also *self*-critique; as a scene in *And Life Goes On …*
makes clear, when a man who acted in *Where Is the Friend's House?*
complains that he'd been made to wear a hump and look and act older
than he was in reality, Kiarostami is acutely aware of the dangers inherent
in the power dynamics of film-making. And despite his disavowal of the
suicidal sentiments in *The Taste of Cherry*, even in that film it's possible,
perhaps, to discern in the protagonist's sense of isolation and self-doubt a
reflection of the rather reclusive Kiarostami's feelings about having
become, with astonishing rapidity, a festival favourite.[103]

Far from simply being self-reflexive, then, the intertextual elements in
Kiarostami's work often render it profoundly political.[104] That said, he has
occasionally been accused of making 'apolitical' films (one suspects there's
confusion here between political film on the one hand and simplistic
humanism or ideological propaganda on the other). Few, however, could
fail to notice the political aspects of *10*; indeed, given the vein of self-
criticism outlined above, one might even view the film as an admission
that here was a subject which needed to be addressed and which, for one
reason or another, had not been dealt with adequately in Kiarostami's
other films. In line with Sabzian's hopes in *Close-Up*, in *10 on Ten*
Kiarostami endorses the Italian neo-realist Cesare Zavattini's theory that
'the first person who comes along could be the subject of your film' – and

that person, of course, might be a woman; or many women; or a ten-year-old boy.

Is there a Kiarostami surrogate in *10*? Since he tends not to make films with single identification figures, and given his comments above on the need for kindred spirits, one gets the impression that – just as the film might depict different aspects of one woman – there's a little of Kiarostami in all the characters, including Amin. But given Mania's dark glasses, the fact that she's always driving (a favourite pastime of the director), and the way she endlessly questions her passengers about their lives, one can only suspect that – for want of a far better phrase – Kiarostami may have been wanting to explore his own feminine side.

(x) The Film
What is *10*?

It's neither reality nor fiction. It's an Oedipal fable, a Socratic dialogue, a political diatribe and a social document. It's almost entirely set within the confines of one car but mainly concerns life outside that car. It might be about one woman or about six women. It's about the power exerted by men, but has only one proper speaking part for a male, and a ten-year-old at that. It's about anger and acceptance. About loving oneself in order to love others. About a city we never really see. It's contemporary yet strangely timeless; unusually intimate and rigorously unsentimental; determinedly prosaic and deeply marked by poetic tropes; quarrelsome and contemplative. It's a film of great formal audacity and sophistication, but it experiments with form only insofar as it serves content. It's made by someone attempting to abandon conventional modes of direction, and as such is clearly the work of perhaps the only major director in the world who'd want to try such a thing, let alone succeed. Quite beautiful in its strange coherence, it's a film of endless ambiguities and countless contradictions. The film never settles …

And the questions keep on coming. Why, for instance, does Mania let the prostitute stay in her car when she gets in by mistake? What can we infer about her own life from the questions she puts to the woman? Why is Mania's voice sometimes not in sync in this scene? Is there significance to the fact that Amin mutters 'sex, sex, sex' to himself (after saying his dad watches porn) in a way that echoes the prostitute claiming she enjoys her work because of the 'sex, love, sex, sex'?[105] What is the timespan of the film meant to be? Could the ten chapters be meaningfully rearranged in a different order? Is it coincidence that *10* was shot the way it was, or, given the now widespread use of surveillance cameras, was that a resonance intended by Kiarostami? Is there a hint of lesbian flirtation when Mania encourages her passenger to remove her veil?[106] And is there any import to be read into Mania telling Amin that, while married to his father, she was 'like a zombie'?

With regard to this last question, perhaps not; after all, Mania is shouting at this stage, enraged by memories of an oppressively possessive husband and of the lies she had to tell simply to regain her freedom through divorce: 'A woman has no right to live! A woman has to die so as to be able to live? I ran away ... I was like a zombie. A zombie!' But perhaps it offers a clue to another way in which 10 grew out of its predecessors; like all the features since *And Life Goes On ...*, it's about life-and-death, or death-in-life, or the struggle of life against death. Because of a chauvinism reflected in and enforced by Iran's laws, women there are forced to live a half-life; as Mania points out to her friend, sobbing because her possessive husband left her: 'We're unhappy, dependent, clinging. When we're little we cling to our mother and father, then to another boy, then to our child; when our child is taken, we cling to our work. What's preventing you from being yourself?' And later: 'We come into the world for that: to win and to lose. Win! Lose! ... Why don't you want to lose? See what it's like!'

Kiarostami's cinema of problems, obstacles, challenges and questions never offers facile solutions; 10 doesn't end with the world changing or Mania finding her situation improved. But it does send her on a journey to 'see what it's like', and she's determined to be herself insofar as life allows. She's no more able to rid herself of oppression against women than she can remove death from the equation with life, but she can at least try to achieve some control, by loving herself rather than remaining, like her friend, complicit in her own suffering. As ever in Kiarostami, it's a matter of attitude: how you look at things and what you do with the information gained.

'I don't have answers. It's like a journey, but also a circle. But it's true the final moment is a little like a dawn coming after the darkness: you finally find that it's maybe not quite so difficult after all ...'[107]

7 A Lesson for Others

Just before writing this book, I interviewed Michael Mann about his new film *Collateral* – about 80 per cent of which, coincidentally, was shot with digital cameras, and long sequences of which are set in a car, which is driven around a sprawling city and contains the driver and one passenger (though there is, again coincidentally, another unseen person behind them – this time dead in the trunk). Before starting the interview proper, we chatted a little, and I mentioned I was about to start work on a book about Kiarostami's *10*. Mann was puzzled. He knew of the director but hadn't heard of the movie. I said it had been shot on digital entirely within a car. He was interested …

In mentioning this, I am certainly not belittling a man I consider to be one of the few real artists still making mature, intelligent and audacious films in Hollywood; though knowledgeable and discerning about movies, Mann's also extremely busy. But it may be revealing of the state of cinema that *10* hadn't appeared on his radar. The film did play in the States, to Hoberman-like raves and Ebert-style rants, but Hollywood and America mostly didn't notice. Why would they when, with the exception of a few folk like Mann, they subscribe to the old, widespread idea of film as industrially produced entertainment with no artistic potential and few socio-political responsibilities? Kiarostami has always worked against that grain,[108] but no film has done so quite as polemically – or with such genuine humility – as *10*. As I hope the preceding pages have proven, the film shows not only that it's possible to make a film with the most modest resources, but that that film, however 'small', may still be astonishingly rich in allusion, resonance, emotional power, political import, dramaturgical nuance and cinematic subtlety.

Follow that car: Mania Akbari in her digital feature *20 Fingers*

Divorce is the biggest problem for families.

How many film-makers will take up the unspoken challenge to follow suit?[109] The most obvious example at time of writing is Mania Akbari's own *20 Fingers*, a fascinating and intelligent if openly derivative digital film in which she and Bijan Daneshmand (the film's producer) act out six seemingly semi-improvised vignettes exploring the troubled politics of male-female relationships; each consists of a single take and (except for a scene shot by a restaurant window with a busy street in the background) takes place in or on some kind of constantly moving vehicle. There will, I'm sure, be other examples. Already in Iran, Kiarostami's influence can perhaps be discerned in a number of films, including some of those by former assistants Jafar Panahi, Bahman Ghobadi (*A Time for Drunken Horses* [*Zamani barayeh masti asbha*, 2000], *Marooned in Iraq* [*Gomgashtei dar Aragh*, 2002], and *Turtles Can Fly* [*Lakposhtha ham parvaz mikonand*, 2004]), and Hassan Yektapanah (*Djomeh* [2000], and *Story Undone* [*Dastan natamam*, 2004]); even Mohsen Makhmalbaf made a Kiarostami-style film with *Moment of Innocence*. In Turkey, meanwhile, something akin to the continuing narrative dynamics of Kiarostami's 'Koker films' can be found in the work of Nuri Bilge Ceylan – *The Small Town* (*Kasaba*, 1998); *Clouds in May* (*Mayis Sikintis*, 1999); and *Distant* (*Uzak*, 2002) – who has spoken openly of his admiration for the Iranian. While none of these directors, apart from Akbari, has yet made anything quite as stylistically austere as *10*, it's still early days; and besides, making a film like *10* does have its budgetary advantages.

Not everyone, of course, will achieve the kind of complexity and nuance found in *10*; as Kiarostami himself wrote in his Cannes press statement: 'Making something simple requires a great deal of experience. And, first of all, you need to understand that simplicity isn't the same as facility.'[110] But then not everyone needs to adopt the extreme minimalism of his methods. They just need to take heart from his experiment having proved, once and for all, that there *is* an alternative for film-makers, less gargantuan in its greed for material resources than the kind of film-making favoured by Hollywood and its imitators;[111] a kind of film-making which operates on a more truly human scale, in which imagination is the prime requisite and resource, not only on the part of the artist but of the viewer, who may participate more actively in the construction of a film's 'meaning'. It's a way forward that looks back to film's roots.

'I don't think cinema needs all these new tools. A camera, three lenses, a couple of tripods will do, just like in the early days of cinema. They made their films with so little.'[112]

8 A Lesson for Kiarostami

A man sits on the shore. In one hand he holds a yogurt, in the other a spoon which he dips into the sea. Another man comes up and asks what he's doing. 'Making a *doog*' – that's a traditional drink we have, made from yogurt and salted water. The other man says, 'You can't make a *doog* from so little yogurt and such a big sea!' 'True,' comes the reply. 'But if I can, what a *doog* it will be!'[113]

In some ways, the Kiarostami film *10* most closely resembles is *Close-Up*. Its subject is contemporary, urban, and intimately related to the personal experiences of various people who mostly 'play' themselves; it concerns social inequality, the inadequacy of the law, and dreams of a better life; its use of ellipsis, omission and changes in point of view makes us repeatedly question the veracity and significance of what we see and hear. It's a film which feels – in Kiarostami's words – 'as if it were making itself'.

On the waterfront: *Five*

Duck soup: *Five*

But while, as we've seen, *10* is organically linked to all the director's earlier work, it also constitutes a turning-point in that the discovery of digital encouraged him to use even more minimalist methods than before. In the statement written for its Cannes premiere, after alluding to a story by Kundera about his father's vocabulary having become limited, in old age, to two words ('It's strange!'), Kiarostami claimed: 'This film is my own "two words". It resumes almost everything [I've done in film].[114] I say "almost" because I'm already thinking about my next film. A one-word film perhaps...'[115]

Indeed. Kiarostami's next works were *10 on Ten* – a minimalist master-class (excepting some clips, the entire film has him driving alone in his car around the roads travelled in *The Taste of Cherry* and addressing a digital camera more or less located in the passenger seat) – and *Five* (2004), an assemblage of five short films shot on the shores of the Caspian. The first depicts a piece of wood tossed by the tide till it breaks in two, at which point the halves drift apart until one exits the frame. The second observes people walking along a promenade, from both left and right, with the sea in the background; eventually two groups of men stop and talk with one another, but then they go their separate ways and the promenade empties of people. The third shows a distant group of dogs on the beach; slowly the sun's light gets so strong that all we can see are little black dots. The fourth (and funniest) has a line of dozens of ducks crossing the beach in front of the camera from left to right ... until one starts hurrying back in the direction whence it came, only to be followed by the entire flock. And the fifth, shot by a pond at night, mostly shows blackness, accompanied by the sound of frogs croaking; at times the moon emerges from behind the clouds to reveal its reflection upon the rippled water; there is also a rainstorm. Finally, the birds begin to sing and the sun comes up.

Five is an extraordinary work and, despite its lack of conventional narrative, entirely in keeping with the overall development of Kiarostami's oeuvre. For one thing, using digital allows him to pursue his dream of 'a one-word film' – each film (except the one that moves a little to follow the wood) appears to consist of one static shot; for another, it allows him to free himself 'of the obligations of narration and the slavery of directing'[116] – the film is a further step in his efforts to eliminate or modify that activity. It is also a sublimely beautiful response to the natural world, taking its place alongside the earlier rural road-movies.

But there's more to it than that. First, despite the lack of a story, the films are far more than just pretty pictures: assembled in order, they comprise a kind of abstract or emotional narrative arc, which moves evocatively from separation and solitude to community, from motion to rest, near-silence to sound and song, light to darkness and back to light again, ending on a note of rebirth and regeneration. Second, they're *not* documentary records; in reality Kiarostami actively influenced what might happen in front of his camera in various ways (tempting dogs and ducks with food, for example), and constructed the final segment from some twenty takes filmed over several months;[117] the soundtrack was also 'composed', almost like a symphony of natural noise, during a four-month mixing process. *Five* is emphatically not a video installation,[118] nor is it purely the product of artless observation; it is *digital cinema*, primarily intended, like most other films, to be watched on a big screen in a darkened room. And it uses many of Kiarostami's usual methods – lies, repetition, long takes, darkness, ellipsis, off-screen sound, invisible cuts, even non-professional actors of various species[119] – to encourage us to look again at the world, a little more patiently and closely, and consider it afresh.

It's very unlikely that Kiarostami will ever only make digital films – his next work, in the portmanteau film *Tickets* (2005), was again shot on 35mm[120] – and even he admits you can't really go beyond single-shot movies ('That's it!'[121]), but at least he is eager to explore new approaches to film-making.

10 showed me that if people are involved with a character or subject, they don't need the other stuff, so it gave me the confidence to make *Five*. Ten years from now, I don't think anyone will be using 35mm; digital is improving almost daily. And if you can use a camera as easily as a pen or paintbrush, film can become more of an art form. Art has to come from one person, or as close to that as possible. With digital, you yourself can be totally responsible for whether the work's good or bad … But you do have to *think* in terms of digital – what it can do – otherwise you might as well use 35mm. What matters is not the tool, but what I see and how I see.[122]

9 Poetry and Motion

These days I feel I'm more of a photographer than a director. At times I think: how can one make a film in which nothing is said? If the images give others the power to interpret them in a way I never suspected, it's better to say nothing and leave the viewer free to imagine everything. By telling a story, you tell *one* story. Every listener … hears one story. But if you say nothing, there's a whole pack of things. The power then passes to the spectator …[123]

For some years now, cinema has not been Kiarostami's only tool in his attempts to help us see the world differently. He has also established himself as a photographer, mainly of landscapes, first in colour and more recently in black and white; he has been exhibited around the world, and collections of his pictures have been published in several books. In terms of the content – winding roads and streams, mountain ranges, fields of crops and flowers, solitary trees on hillsides, thick forests, sculpted clouds in enormous skies, and the occasional small animal or human – the photographs are obviously closer to his rural films and *Five* (which, lacking narrative, visible cuts and a mobile camera, has been likened to moving photographs) than to urban films like *10*. That said, in terms of form *10* and the photographs are, on close inspection, clearly the work of the same man.

Like the films, the photos make a virtue of repetition, rhyme and concealment. The latter reveal countless, literally endless zigzag paths, tracks and roads disappearing around mountains, over hillsides or dropping into hidden valleys.[124] A tree may be seen only in its reflection in a pond;[125] another is visible only because its top peeks over the crest of a hill, its bulk hidden on the other side.[126] Some compositions look so flattened[127] as to give an impression of near-abstraction;[128] others discover strange, almost cohesive shapes made up of a diversity of elements, such as cloud, trees and soil.[129] Some play with darkness and light, particularly in the shadows created by clouds;[130] others explore a range of similarities in colour (such as the different greens of a tree in a hillside field)[131] or degrees of contrast in colour and texture (orange poppies in grass; lush pastures and empty skies).[132] In the black-and-white pictures, especially, snow figures heavily, often contrasted with the shapes and shadows of trees, or crows.[133] Horizontal, vertical and diagonal features are balanced with careful precision. There is always a sense of harmonious proportion, creating a deceptive impression of simplicity. In fact, although Kiarostami avoids using filters and a multiplicity of lenses and prefers to interfere with the image as

little as possible in the printing process, much thought goes into producing these pictures. He has contemplated the beauty of the natural world and, through his photographs, invites us to contemplate that beauty, too.

But how does this relate to the world of *10*? The clue lies in poetry. Hamid Dabashi is not alone in having noted the importance of poetry to Iranians in general and to Kiarostami in particular;[134] not only did poetry shape Kiarostami's cinematic sensibility, but he became a poet himself. I cannot vouch for the accuracy of claims made by Ahmad Karimi-Hakkak and Michael Beard, translators of his volume of verse *Walking with the Wind*, that he 'may be called the most radical Iranian poet of his generation, perhaps of the century';[135] I can, however, confirm that Kiarostami's brief, almost *haiku*-like poems are very closely related to his photography and films. For one thing, the poems are very often concerned with (our or someone else's) acts of seeing and hearing:

An old villager / on the mountain path – / a young man's call from afar.[136]

Indeed, many are concerned with the relationship between visibility and invisibility:

It grew larger and larger. / It grew full / and turned smaller and smaller.

Tonight / a moonless night.[137]

They deal with gradations of likeness:

One hundred obedient soldiers / enter the barracks / early on a moonlit night.

Rebellious dreams![138]

And with contrast:

A woman in labour / awake / surrounded by five girls and a sleeping man.[139]

They make startling, zigzagging play with point of view:

How merciful / that the turtle doesn't see / the little bird's effortless flight.[140]

And besides reflecting the formal devices used in the films and photography, they sometimes encroach upon the same territory in terms of content:

The dog lies in ambush / at the end of the alley / for the new beggar.[141]

The use of corresponding or oppositional images to explore different modes of existence is found in classical Persian poets like Rumi, Hafez or Khayyam; the love of nature may be found in Sepehri, the sense of the distances between people in Forough.[142] Kiarostami is consciously working within a tradition in each and every art form he has elected to work in – he has even recently turned his attention to the theatre, with a partly filmic staging of the traditional Persian passion play, the *Ta'ziyeh*, in Rome and Taormina, in the summer of 2003 – but he is also happy to experiment with traditions. Of the many elements shared by his films, photographs, poems and even, perhaps, his paintings,[143] two things are paramount: a sense that the world, in all its everyday banality, has its wonders and beauties and mysteries; and the insistence that it is therefore worthy of contemplation.

It's precisely this kind of interaction Kiarostami is inviting us to enter into with all his work, *10* included. In *10 on Ten*, he says he's uninterested in false climaxes and guessing games; it's ambiguity that's important, which is why he doesn't believe 'a film is to be understood. Do we understand a piece of music, a painting or the exact meaning of a poem?' For Kiarostami close observation is not about inspecting every little twist in the plot, as some do with mind-bending puzzle films like *The Usual Suspects*, *Memento* or *Mulholland Dr.*[144] (his films don't have enough plot for that kind of attention, anyway); it's a more interactive relationship that he has in mind. It's about venturing into a film's open or empty spaces, and bringing your own imagination, personality and experience into play with whatever you find there. Thus, simplicity makes for complexity, omission for plenitude. Just as there's more to a poem than words on a page, and more to music than the notes actually played, so a film may reveal far more than what we may be told through a mere story.

Light the fire and I'll show you something,
Something invisible if you don't wish to see it,
Something which cannot be heard if you don't wish to listen to its breath.[145]

10 Conclusion: The Start of Something Big?

It's really a question of using your camera like a pen, not just as an instrument for commercial purposes. It's about how you look at life. How you fix your eyes on a neighbour, a landscape, a friend, your brother, children, everyone … it's all a matter of concentration. If you concentrate, you can find something more. If you don't, you won't get it.[146]

As we saw at the beginning of this book, some people don't get *10*. This book was written partly because the author feels, with all due respect, that it's worth taking a long, close look at *10*, its maker and his other films. If you're going to 'get' *10*, or indeed most of his work, especially since *And Life Goes On …* , it's worth devoting the same kind of attention to what Kiarostami's trying to do as he routinely devotes to his subjects. His gaze is sympathetic without being sentimental, compassionate but never condescending; it takes in a great deal of information about the subject, including how a gaze is returned: how do his subjects see him? What are his responsibilities to them? What is their exact relationship? As a film-maker, will he inevitably, somehow, betray them? At least he's asking those questions, which puts him on the right track. Maybe he was a little late, as he's admitted, in getting around to making a film about women, but at least he eventually did it – and made, in this writer's opinion, a masterpiece.

There are some, however, who do feel betrayed – not those he's made films with and about, but others who seem to resent his international standing and imply that the 'festival favourite' must be selling out. The idiocy of this position is evident as soon as one considers the development of his oeuvre. Why would anyone keep making such challenging, contrary, *different* films if he or she were mainly concerned with fame and fortune? Kiarostami is an unusually restless artist, curious about the world and how he can explore it in his art, and reluctant to be categorised or constrained, either by others or by his own reputation. He's always been his own man (this probably, ironically, a consequence both of his having originally been state-funded and of his not being much of a cinephile). Even at the time of the Revolution, he had his own agenda, making films about the ethics of being an informer and on how to look after your teeth:[147]

His persistent attempt to show us how to look differently … sketches out a mode of being that survives all the pains and promises of a revolution … His cinema is the vision of life on earth, certainty in the real, a celebration of the transitory …[148]

No wonder his work has been described as 'unusually careless – free – on the question of audience.'[149]

It's in this light that *10* should be understood: as one more step on a zigzagging path of exploration that's led him from his very first film to *Five* and beyond.[150] There's a strong sense of continuity ('There are similarities between *Bread and Alley* and *10*, especially in the long, fixed shots and the way of telling a story; there's a simplicity to both, I think'),[151] and one of the most consistent aspects of Kiarostami's work is his eagerness to keep moving. His art is like Heraclitus' river: always changing, always the same. And each time you return to dip your toes in, you notice something new.

Such paradoxes are an integral part of his work, as we've seen; this whole book, in a way, has been concerned with how such a 'small' film can contain so many riches, and how a film which was the result of an attempt to eliminate 'direction' is so clearly the work of its creator. In a sense, however many times we may have watched and listened to and thought about the film, what we're left with is still … questions. And in the long term that's far more rewarding than being wowed by a film's flashy technique, stars, special effects or marketing campaign.

Because Kiarostami keeps moving forwards and changing tack, he's always a few steps ahead of us. It's too soon to know what influence, if any, *10* will have on the film-making world, but its example is there, demonstrating that films that matter – films that are socially, politically, ethically, philosophically and aesthetically relevant, serious, important, intelligible and accessible – can be made in much the same way as a book, a painting, a sculpture or piece of music. And because *10* is part of Kiarostami's organic, continuing creative process, if you keep on looking at it, with concentration and care, it will almost certainly grow.

Notes

1 Interview with the author at National Film Theatre, London, June 1999.
2 Interview with Farah Nayeri in *Sight and Sound*, vol. 3 no. 12 (NS), December 1993, p. 27.
3 Godfrey Cheshire, 'How to Read Kiarostami', *Cineaste* vol. 25 no. 4, pp. 8–15.
4 *Chicago Sun-Times*, 11 April 2003.
5 *Sight and Sound*, vol. 12 no. 10, October 2002, pp. 30–2. I should add that my mention of Ebert's review here is certainly not an attempt to 'get back' at him, as I didn't feel my critical reputation, such as it is, was in any way damaged by his words. His review merely serves as a good example of the kind of 'emperor's new clothes' charges sometimes directed against Kiarostami's films.
6 David Thomson, *The New Biographical Dictionary of Film* (London: Little, Brown, 2002), pp. 466–7.
7 Azadeh Farahmand, 'Perspectives on Recent (International Acclaim for) Iranian Cinema', in Richard Tapper (ed.), *The New Iranian Cinema: Politics, Representation and Identity* (London: I. B. Tauris, 2002), pp. 86ff.
8 For the record, in my opinion the other contenders are *Close-Up*, *And Life Goes On …*, 1992) and *The Wind Will Carry Us*, 1999), with *The Taste of Cherry* and *Five* close behind, which may reflect how profound are the connections between the films, and how individual titles are perhaps best viewed as steps in one continuing artistic project.
9 As we shall see later, with somewhat characteristic perversity, instead of using the 'clout' that accompanied these extremely prestigious international prizes to make bigger movies, or even to make more of the same, Kiarostami took the opportunity afforded by his high profile to make 'smaller', more experimental and even less 'mainstream' work.
10 Jonathan Rosenbaum, *Movie Wars* (London: Wallflower, 2002).
11 Interview with the author, Victoria and Albert Museum, London, January 2004.
12 Jonathan Rosenbaum and Mehrnaz Saeed-Vafa, *Abbas Kiarostami* (Urbana and Chicago: University of Illinois Press, 2003).
13 Elements of these charges may be found both in Farahmand, 'Perspectives on Recent (International Acclaim for) Iranian Cinema', and in Chris Darke's comments on *10* in a website article he wrote in November 2001 on surveillance in the cinema. 'Letter from London', <www.sensesofcinema.com/contents/03/25/letter_london.html>
14 Godfrey Cheshire, 'Abbas Kiarostami: Seeking a Home', in John Boorman and Walter Donohue (eds), *Projections 8* (London: Faber and Faber, 1998), p. 226.
15 Hamid Naficy, 'Islamizing Film Culture in Iran: A Post-Khatami Update', in Tapper, *The New Iranian Cinema*, p. 30.
16 Mehrnaz Saeed-Vafa in Rosenbaum and Saeed-Vafa, *Abbas Kiarostami*, p. 56.
17 Hamid Dabashi, *Close-Up: Iranian Cinema, Past, Present and Future* (London: Verso, 2001), pp. 14ff.
18 Hamid Naficy, 'Iranian Cinema', in Rose Issa and Sheila Whitaker (eds), *Life and Art: The New Iranian Cinema* (London: National Film Theatre, 1999), p. 19.
19 Ibid., p. 20.
20 Hamid Naficy, 'Islamizing Film Culture in Iran' in Tapper, *The New Iranian Cinema*, pp. 36–7.
21 Ibid., pp. 46–7.
22 Quoted in Hamid Naficy, 'Veiled Vision/Powerful Presences: Women in Post-Revolutionary Iranian Cinema', in Issa and Whitaker, *Life and Art*, p. 58.
23 Naficy, 'Islamizing Film Culture in Iran', in Tapper, *The New Iranian Cinema*, pp. 51–2.
24 Many written testimonies to Kiarostami's importance (admittedly translated into Greek) may be found in Nikos Savvatis (ed.), *Kiarostami* (Athens: Kastaniotis, 2004), pp 128–34; most of the other film-makers mentioned have spoken of their admiration for Kiarostami at one time or another to the author himself.

25 Quoted in 'Trente questions à Abbas Kiarostami par Michel Ciment', in *Abbas Kiarostami: Photographies, Photographs, Fotografie* … (Paris: Hazan, 1999), pp. 8–9.
26 Alberto Elena, *Abbas Kiarostami* (Madrid: Catedra, 2002), p. 18.
27 Rosenbaum has compared the didactic films Kiarostami made for Kanun to Brecht's *Lehrstücken*, or learning plays, and rightly questions whether his films about children were actually made *for* children; Rosenbaum and Saeed-Vafa, *Abbas Kiarostami*, p. 9.
28 Whether we are meant to interpret this nightmare as the boy's fear of punishment for his misdeeds or as the result of a (perhaps typical) unhappy childhood is left intriguingly unclear by Kiarostami, but given the treatment of children by adults in some of his later films, I feel we should not discount the latter option.
29 Rosenbaum and Saeed-Vafa, *Abbas Kiarostami*, p. 11.
30 Elena, *Abbas Kiarostami*, p. 105.
31 Kiarostami was perverse but right not to let us know for sure whether the boys were definitely alive or not; after all, why should their lives matter more than all the others affected by the earthquake, just because they had appeared in his film? It is surely enough that the director learns they are *probably* alive; besides, the genuinely curious will find out for themselves that they have survived, since they appear briefly in Kiarostami's next film.
32 Kiarostami himself has often admitted to a reluctance to group the films this way.
33 The other Palme d'or-winner was *The Eel* (*Unagi*) by Japan's Shohei Imamura.
34 Notably *Jaham Nama Palace* (*Kaaj-e Jahan-Nama*, 1977) and *Dinner for One* (*Sham-e yeknafare*), from the compilation *Lumière and Company*, 1995.
35 Rosenbaum and Saeed-Vafa, *Abbas Kiarostami*, p. 38.
36 Ibid., p. 59.
37 Kiarostami has admitted to the author that, while he did witness a storm of amazing force

during his stay in Uganda, what we see/hear is actually a dramatic reconstruction.
38 Interview with the author, Victoria and Albert Museum, London, January 2003.
39 Ibid.
40 Interview with the author, Cannes, May 2002.
41 Interview with the author, London, September 2002.
42 Interview with the author, London, January 2004.
43 Interview with the author, London, September 2002.
44 In one interview, Kiarostami said he had an earphone placed beneath Akbari's veil so that he could occasionally make suggestions about where to take the conversation. See Alberto Barbera and Elisa Resegotti (eds), *Kiarostami* (Milan: Electra, 2003), p. 193. But when I asked him about this (in London, September, 2004), he said he had only a vague recollection of having tried it just once; he'd found it either unnecessary or unhelpful.
45 Interview with the author, Turin, September 2003.
46 Interview with the author, Cannes, May 2002.
47 Watching the film very closely, one can occasionally detect some slight movement, but that is presumably the result of camera shake or of editing different takes together.
48 In Rosenbaum and Saeed-Vafa, *Abbas Kiarostami*, p. 101, Saeed-Vafa postulates that Kiarostami may have used the sound of a bell because he had likened his role as director on this film to that of a football coach, doing most of his work before a game starts. But Kiarostami has confirmed to the author that he chose the sound because many of the driver's dialogues (especially those with her son) are quite combative; it's as if she's in for another round.
49 As far as I am able to judge, of the characters actually seen travelling in the car, these are the only two whose names are heard in the film. They are also, of course, the

names of the actors in question. For the sake of clarity I use the name Mania when referring to the character in the film, and Akbari when referring to the actress.

50 Not that they would be able to do so even if they did feel such a need; as we have seen, Kiarostami denied them the possibility of ever knowing such details, mainly because he had not yet worked them out for himself.

51 Often, when filming with the boy, Kiarostami and Akbari would collect him a little late so that he was already in a bad mood when they started shooting.

52 For this reason, I do not feel that the chapter 'headings', with their numbers and bells, are primarily intended as distancing devices as Rosenbaum claims (Rosenbaum and Saeed-Vafa, *Abbas Kiarostami*, p. 100). True, they remind us we are watching a film, but given how it was shot and assembled, it's hard to see how Kiarostami could have found any properly convincing and seamless transitions with which to stitch together the various segments.

53 Other notable instances include the old woman's hand passing her rosary to Mania, and Mania's hand touching Amin's brow when she asks if he is feverish.

54 Interview with the author, London, January 2004.

55 Interview with the author, Turin, September 2003.

56 Interview with the author, London, January 2004.

57 Amin's father, played by a photographer friend of Kiarostami, is shown only briefly in long shot and shouts only a few basic instructions when Mania collects the boy from him.

58 Interview with the author, London, September 2002.

59 Interview with the author, London, January 2004.

60 In reality, Mania Akbari (b. 1974) began painting in 1991, and has been exhibited in a number of exhibitions. Since appearing in *10*,

she has also started working as a video artist, and directed the documentary *Crystal* (2003) and *20 Fingers*, a feature profoundly influenced by *10* which premiered in September 2004 at the Venice Film Festival, winning the prize in the digital cinema competition.

61 I was told by one Iranian woman that the language in this scene is authentically crude.

62 Interview with the author, Turin, September 2003.

63 Farahmand, 'Perspectives on Recent (International Acclaim for) Iranian Cinema', in Tapper, *The New Iranian Cinema*, pp. 99–100.

64 Rosenbaum and Saeed-Vafa, *Abbas Kiarostami*, p. 68.

65 Interview with the author, National Film Theatre, London, June 1999.

66 This is implied not only by the woman's voice but by the fact that Mania does ask, with a note of some incredulity, how old she is – to which she signally fails to respond.

67 Interview with the author, London, September 2002.

68 Catalogue for the Sélection Officielle, Festival de Cannes 2002, p. 50; also the MK2 press book.

69 'I very soon forgot about the camera; I knew it was filming, but the advantage of digicams is that they intrude so little.' Interview with the author, London, September 2002.

70 Interview with the author, London, January 2004.

71 According to Akbari: 'Only men have the right kind of clippers, but women aren't allowed into men's barbershops, so Abbas and my husband had to shave her head in a van.' Interview with the author, London, September 2002.

72 Naficy, 'Veiled Vision/Powerful Presences, in Issa and Whitaker, *Life and Art*, pp. 48ff.

73 If anyone doubts the inferior status legally afforded women by the Islamic Republic, a passage from Elaine Sciolino's *Persian Mirrors* (New York: The Free Press, 2000), p. 115, may be persuasive: 'Women do not serve as judges or religious leaders. Adultery is still punishable by stoning to death. Polygamy is legal. In a divorce, fathers control custody of sons over the age of two and daughters over the age of seven … Men can divorce their wives at will, but women need to prove that their spouses are insane, impotent, violent or unable to support the family … A woman's testimony in court has half the weight of a man's. Women can be arrested for … exposing their heads and necks and the curves of their bodies in public.'

74 Hence the authorities' refusal to allow the film to be shown uncut in Iran.

75 Interview with the author, London, January 2004.

76 Stephen Bransford, in an excellent essay devoted to Kiarostami's earlier films, argues that: 'Kiarostami's dedication to the representation of "exterior" Iranian life doesn't mean that his characters aren't preoccupied with what's happening indoors.' Bransford, 'Days in the Country: Representations of Rural Space and Place in Kiarostami's *Life and Nothing More*, *Through the Olive Trees* and *The Wind Will Carry Us*', on <www.sensesofcinema.com>.

77 In this respect *10* bears a surprising resemblance to George Cukor's *The Women* (1939), from which men are wholly absent but in which they are endlessly discussed.

78 J. Hoberman, 'Formal Attire', *Village Voice*, 5 March 2003, p. 113.

79 See Elena, *Abbas Kiarostami*, pp. 105ff.

80 Bransford, 'Days in the Country', p. 7.

81 Interview with the author, Cannes, May 2002.

82 Indeed, apart from Amin himself, these two men are the very last people we see in the entire film, though I am not sure we should attach too much significance to that fact.

83 This not only ties in with the theme of sisterhood, but lends force to the argument that all the women seen in the film may be viewed as different ages or aspects of one woman.

84 Interview with the author, Cannes, May 2002.

85 Interview with the author, London, January 2004.

86 Interview with the author, Turin, September 2003.

87 MK2 press notes.

88 Rosenbaum and Saeed-Vafa, *Abbas Kiarostami*, pp. 66–7.

89 Providing that we, like the café proprietress in *The Wind Will Carry Us*, remember that a woman's work is never done.

90 Rosenbaum and Saeed-Vafa, *Abbas Kiarostami*, p. 66.

91 In *10 on Ten* Kiarostami uses this argument to explain his preference for not using music in films before the closing credits.

92 Interview with the author, Cannes, May 2002.

93 Interview with the author, London, January 2004.

94 Interview with the author, Cannes, May 2002.

95 Rosenbaum, in Rosenbaum and Saeed-Vafa, *Abbas Kiarostami*, p. 30.

96 In the Japanese documentary *A Week with Kiarostami* (Yuji Mohara, 1999), shot on the set of *The Wind Will Carry Us*, we see Kiarostami himself speaking the dialogue for a member of the protagonist's TV crew, concealed at the time from the camera in what in the film is supposed to be a guesthouse bedroom.

97 Interview with the author, Cannes, May 2002.

98 Naficy, 'Veiled Vision/Powerful Presences', in Issa and Whitaker, *Life and Art*, p. 49.

99 Rosenbaum and Saeed-Vafa, *Abbas Kiarostami*, p. 58.

100 Interview with the author, National Film Theatre, London, June 1999.

101 In notes written about his theatrical production of the *Ta'ziyeh* in Rome in 2003, Kiarostami wrote: 'When we speak of war, we always think about bombing. But there is another war, an interior one: the struggle between rich and poor. It's there always, a silent war, bound to the question of survival' (author's translation). Kiarostami, 'Dal cinema al teatro (e ritorno)' ('From cinema to theatre – and back again'), in Barbera and Resegotti, *Kiarostami*, p. 205.

102 Rosenbaum and Saeed-Vafa, *Abbas Kiarostami*, p. 37.

103 While I think Godfrey Cheshire ('How to Read Kiarostami', pp. 12–13), pushes this argument too forcefully, and find a little far-fetched his comments about the self-critical aspects of *The Traveller*, in 'Abbas Kiarostami: Seeking a Home' he is clearly correct in stressing the autobiographical dimensions of Kiarostami's work overall.

104 Bransford's essay is especially effective in examining how Kiarostami's films deal with class and the distance between the film-maker and his subjects. Bransford, 'Days in the Country'.

105 Kiarostami has told me that the resemblance of Amin's words and manner of speaking to those he'd written for the girl playing the prostitute was in fact purely coincidental.

106 Some of these questions are raised by Rosenbaum and Saeed-Vafa in their dialogue about the film (*Abbas Kiarostami*, pp. 99ff.); for the record, while I'd agree that Kiarostami plays with our expectations of possible homosexual desire at the start of *The Taste of Cherry*, I don't feel there are serious lesbian overtones in chapter (2), despite some banter between the prostitute and Mania in the earlier scene.

107 Interview with the author, London, January 2004.

108 Godfrey Cheshire has written that 'his work amounts to an implicit critique and rejection of most cinema, which trades in identification, sensation and catharsis'. Cheshire, 'How to Read Kiarostami', p. 15.

109 In *10 on Ten*, Kiarostami takes care to remind viewers that he is self-taught and that, if they want success, they should follow the American formulas (at which point he leaves

his car to urinate – off-screen, of course – at the side of the road, before turning his digital camera, in another display of its potential, to give us a close-up of a busy ants' nest).

110 MK2 press notes.

111 Kiarostami has noted, with regard to another film that happened to have made extensive use of digital technology: 'The film was in competition in Cannes, the same day that the new *Star Wars* was screened. We made a calculation: my entire film cost the same as ten frames of Lucas's film.' Barbera and Resegotti, *Kiarostami*, p. 190.

112 Kiarostami in *10 on Ten*.

113 Interview with the author, Cannes, May 2003.

114 Interpretative words supplied by the author.

115 MK2 press notes.

116 MK2 press notes for *10 on Ten* and *Five*.

117 'This was necessary because of the movements of the moon and clouds; I could only shoot for about five minutes between around eleven and one. I drove about 3,000 km just to shoot that twenty-five minutes; fortunately there was no producer to tell me not to bother!' Interview with the author, Cannes, May 2004.

118 'I resist the term video art, which is going in a different direction from my work. I'm trying to eliminate myself from the work, not to impose my vision on the viewer, but a video artist plans, designs and shoots exactly according to what he or she wants to say. I don't really want to say anything.' Interview with the author, Victoria and Albert Museum, London, January 2004.

119 The dogs' wagging tails, conspicuous in what Kiarostami has called 'maybe my first love story', take us back to *Bread and Alley*, highlighting the continuity underlying the progress of his career.

120 The film – which also has episodes by Ermanno Olmi and Ken Loach – was being edited as the writing of this book was in its final stages, and had its premiere in Berlin in February 2005. Kiarostami's episode is certainly a return to narrative of sort, and features some very funny comedy, but it is perhaps most interesting for its play with visibility and invisibility, and its enigmatic hints at various bigger 'stories' external to the episode itself.

121 Interview with the author, London, January 2004.

122 Interview with the author, London, January 2004.

123 (Author's translation.) Kiarostami in Barbera and Resegotti, *Kiarostami*, p. 56.

124 See *Abbas Kiarostami: Photo Collection* (Tehran: Iranian Art Publishing, 2000), and *Abbas Kiarostami: Photographies, Photographs, Fotografie …*, passim.

125 *Abbas Kiarostami: Photographies, Photographs, Fotografie …*, p. 35.

126 Ibid., p. 51.

127 The shallow perspective may reveal the influence of classical Persian miniature-painting, which may also explain the occasional use of perpendicular, low-relief compositions in many of Kiarostami's earlier films (not to mention those of other Iranian directors).

128 *Abbas Kiarostami: Photo Collection*, pp. 121, 173, 181.

129 *Abbas Kiarostami: Photographies, Photographs, Fotografie …*, p. 62.

130 Ibid., pp. 72–4.

131 *Abbas Kiarostami: Photo Collection*, pp. 55–9.

132 Ibid, pp. 71–9.

133 See Barbera and Resegotti, *Kiarostami*, pp. 15–51 and pp. 101–21.

134 Dabashi, *Close-Up*, pp. 40ff.

135 Abbas Kiarostami, *Walking with the Wind*, trans. Ahmad Karimi-Hakkak and Michael Beard (Cambridge, MA: Harvard University Press, 2001), p. 8.

136 Ibid., p. 69.

137 Ibid., p. 51.

138 Ibid., p. 24.

139 Ibid., p. 82.

140 Ibid., p. 44.

141 Ibid., p. 109.

142 Ibid., pp. 8–13.

143 Two of Kiarostami's remarkably detailed paintings of nature can be found reproduced in Barbera and Resegotti, *Kiarostami*, pp. 202–3.

144 Films directed, respectively, by Bryan Singer (1995), Christopher Nolan (2000) and David Lynch (2001).

145 Japanese *haiku* quoted by Kiarostami at the end of *10 on Ten*, as he turns his digital camera towards an ants' nest.

146 Interview with the author, Turin, September 2003.

147 The short *Toothache* (*Dandan-e dard*), 1979.

148 Dabashi, *Close-Up*, p. 59.

149 Cheshire, 'Abbas Kiarostami', in Boorman and Donohue, *Projections 8*, p. 220.

150 Kiarostami has told me of various ideas he's had for the follow-up to *Tickets* – though they all differ from one another in many respects, each idea does seem to grow, one way or another, out of his episode for the portmanteau film. *Plus ça change …*

151 Interview with the author, Turin, September 2003.

Credits

10

France/Iran
2002

Directed by
Abbas Kiarostami
Screenplay by
Abbas Kiarostami
Director of Photography
Abbas Kiarostami
Edited by
Abbas Kiarostami

©2002 MK2 s.a./Abbas
Kiarostami
Production Company
Marin Karmitz and Abbas
Kiarostami present
Made by
Abbas Kiarostami, Mania
Akbari, Roya Arabshahi,
Katayoun Taleizadeh,
Mandana Sharbaf, Amene
Moradi, Amin Maher, Kamran
Adl, Nazanin Joneydi, Mitra
Farahani, Bahman Kiarostami,
Mastaneh Mohajer, Reza
Yazdani, Morteza Tabatabai,
Peyman Yazdanian,
Christophe Rezai, Mazdak
Sepanlou, Ali Boustan. Negar
Rayhani, Noushien Agah,
Ahmad Ansari, Negin Rahimi,
Vahid Ghazi Mirsayid, Ciball
Honar Studio, Nathalie
Kreuther
Soundtrack
"Walking in the Air" by Howard
Blake ©Chester Music Limited
represented by Première
Music Group

Cast
Mania Akbari
Mania, the driver
Amin Maher
Amin, Mania's son
Roya Arabshahi
Katayoun Taleizadeh
Mandana Sharbaf
Amene Moradi
Kamran Adl

8,351 feet
92 minutes 48 seconds

In Colour
DTS

Credits compiled by Markuu
Salmi

Also Published

Amores Perros
Paul Julian Smith (2003)

L'Argent
Kent Jones (1999)

Blade Runner
Scott Bukatman (1997)

Blue Velvet
Michael Atkinson (1997)

Caravaggio
Leo Bersani & Ulysse Dutoit
(1999)

A City of Sadness
Bérénice Reynaud (2002)

Crash
Iain Sinclair (1999)

The Crying Game
Jane Giles (1997)

Dead Man
Jonathan Rosenbaum
(2000)

**Dilwale Dulhaniya Le
Jayenge**
Anupama Chopra (2002)

Don't Look Now
Mark Sanderson (1996)

Do the Right Thing
Ed Guerrero (2001)

Easy Rider
Lee Hill (1996)

The Exorcist
Mark Kermode (1997,
2nd edn 1998,
rev. 2nd edn 2003)

Eyes Wide Shut
Michel Chion (2002)

Groundhog Day
Ryan Gilbey (2004)

Heat
Nick James (2002)

The Idiots
John Rockwell (2003)

Independence Day
Michael Rogin (1998)

Jaws
Antonia Quirke (2002)

L.A. Confidential
Manohla Dargis (2003)

Last Tango in Paris
David Thompson (1998)

The Matrix
Joshua Clover (2004)

**Nosferatu – Phantom der
Nacht**
S.S. Prawer (2004)

**Once Upon a Time in
America**
Adrian Martin (1998)

Pulp Fiction
Dana Polan (2000)

The Right Stuff
Tom Charity (1997)

**Saló or The 120 Days of
Sodom**
Gary Indiana (2000)

Seven
Richard Dyer (1999)

**The Shawshank
Redemption**
Mark Kermode (2003)

The Silence of the Lambs
Yvonne Tasker (2002)

The Terminator
Sean French (1996)

Thelma & Louise
Marita Sturken (2000)

The Thing
Anne Billson (1997)

The Thin Red Line
Michel Chion (2004)

**The 'Three Colours'
Trilogy**
Geoff Andrew (1998)

Titanic
David M. Lubin (1999)

Trainspotting
Murray Smith (2002)

Unforgiven
Edward Buscombe (2004)

The Usual Suspects
Ernest Larsen (2002)

The Wings of the Dove
Robin Wood (1999)

Withnail & I
Kevin Jackson (2004)

**Women on the Verge of a
Nervous Breakdown**
Peter William Evans (1996)

**WR – Mysteries of the
Organism**
Raymond Durgnat (1999)

BFI Publishing
21 Stephen Street
FREEPOST 7
LONDON
W1E 4AN